Speaking Against Fear and Limiting Beliefs

A Practical Guide with Strategies to Overcome Limitations using Biblical Principles

OMOLOLA S. LAWAL

Copyright © 2023 by Omolola Lawal.

MOTIVATION CHAMPS PUBLISHING

Printed and Electronic Versions
ISBN: 978-1-956353-44-0
ISBN (eBook): 978-1-956353-45-7
(Omolola S. Lawal / Motivation Champs)

Cover Designed by Laura Edgerly

Scripture quotations are taken from the Holy Bible.

Scripture taken from the New King James Version®.
Copyright © 1982 by Thomas Nelson. Used by permission.
All rights reserved.

Scripture quotations marked KJV are taken from King James Version.
Public domain.

Scripture quotations marked NLT are taken from the
Holy Bible, New Living Translation, copyright © 1996, 2004.

2015 by Tyndale House Foundation.
Used by permission of Tyndale House Publishers, Inc.,
Carol Stream, Illinois 60188. All rights reserved.

THE HOLY BIBLE, NEW INTERNATIONAL VERSION®, NIV®
Copyright © 1973, 1978, 1984, 2011 by Biblica, Inc.®
Used by permission. All rights reserved worldwide.

Scripture quotations taken from the Amplified Bible (AMP),
Copyright 2015 by The Lockman Foundation.
Used by permission. Lockman.org

Scripture quotations taken from the Amplified Bible (AMPC),
Copyright 1954, 1958, 1962, 1964, 1965, 1987 by The Lockman Foundation Used by permission. Lockman.org

Scripture quotations marked TPT are from The Passion Translation. Copyright 2017, 2018, 2020 by Passion & Fire Ministries, Inc.
Used by permission. All rights reserved. ThePassionTranslation.com.

All rights reserved. No part of this book may be reproduced or transmitted in any form or by any means, electronic or mechanical, including photocopying, recording, or by any information storage and retrieval system, without permission in writing from the copyright owner.

The book was printed in the United States of America.

Special discount may apply on bulk quantities. Please contact Motivation Champs Publishing to order. www.motivationchamps.com

Foreword

Speaking Against Fear and Limiting Beliefs.........

is a book of Personal testimony. Personal testimony is the most effective tool for evangelism. Stating where you were in your faith journey. and where you are now, and what led to the difference, provides a practical demonstration of the power that brings change.

Now, 'power' always follows testimony. Certainly, of course, it is the Blood of the Lamb that redeems people, setting them free from slavery to sin, from slavery to fear! (Revelations 12, the 11th verse,). But when the Record of God's activity is revealed in a personal testimony, there is an unmistakable shift, that brings in something of heaven to the situation to which the Testimony is spoken! In effect, there is a definite anointing that follows when a testimony is shared for the sole purpose of glorifying God.

Such an unmistakable occasion in the Bible, is found in the story of David and Goliath. Read again yourself the testimony of David before Saul the King, in 1 Samuel 17:34 -51. David watched king Saul and his people, the people of God, paralyzed by fear, recalls times in his past during which fear would have paralyzed him himself, but for his belief in the Covenant, that The God of Israel had with His people and took hold of the Promise of God in that Covenant. The anointing upon that Testimony brought down the Power to defeat the enemy. Such is the power that is recorded in this book of Testimony.

However, let us pause here to recall a few things. By the time this book of personal Testimony starts, the writer had come to recognize the voice of the Holy Spirit. In her walk with God, she had come to depend on the leading of The Holy Spirit. It is important for the reader to know this. Otherwise, a cursory observer might treat this as a book of charms: if you begin to chant certain words of The Bible repeatedly, then you will get the results you crave.

No. You must first have a change of identity. You must give your life to Another. You must put off your 'flesh' identity and put on the identity of Christ. You must arrive in a place where God's desire is now your desire, a place where you can now say like Paul, "I no longer live……the life I live in the body I live by faith in the son of God who loved me and gave Himself up for me." Galatians 2:20

You might ask; How do I arrive there? The answer is in your hands in this book. And also contained in the testimonials given by those who have followed on the path illustrated in this book. See the appendices

Speaking Against Fear, is a most readable book, written in a conversational, easy to read style. The style takes the reader on a journey with the writer pausing appropriately from time to time to catch breath and then to continue. And when you get to the end, you feel you cannot stop; you want to continue on the journey, perhaps take someone else with you and certainly in the Company of the Holy Spirit.

Please get hold of this book, a beautifully written illustration of the Beauty of Life that is being lived in the Spirit.

Rev. Dr. Andrew Omotoso. BA (London); MA. Ed.D. (Columbia); M.Div. DMin. (Nyack)

Formerly Registrar, University of Lagos; Formerly Registrar State University of New York at FIT; Emeritus Minister of Christian Education, Bethel Gospel Assembly Harlem New York; President, The Encouragers Ministry www.theencouragers.org

Endorsements

This book "Speaking Against Fear and Limiting Beliefs..." by Omolola S Lawal is a great piece of work that looks at combination of Biblical Scriptures and Practical Solutions to address the subject matter. I am extremely impressed with the opportunity the book affords readers to identity their challenges, look for relevant Bible verses, internalize the Bible verses and speak God's Word over the challenges.

The practicality of this book offers readers through it's work- book format section valuable opportunities to write down steps and actions people will be taking to address the issues of the subject matter.

In my view, the writer's combination of scriptures and practical solutions based on the experience of the Author as a Christian, Counselor, Professional and Practitioner who has engaged with real people, with real needs and has provided real solutions that have helped people already was demonstrated in this book. Documenting the points that have helped and keeps helping deal with their fears and limiting belief in this book is a blessing to people.

Based on what the book contains, which I have only highlighted a fraction of it. I say a Job well done to the Author Omolola S Lawal and want to recommend this book to people around the World as a relevant book for all irrespective of their age, color, race, etc.

Enjoy this book and feel free to recommend it to others.

Pastor Temitayo Olugbenga Okutubo
(Aka Pastor Bubble In Christ). *United Kingdom.*

It can be difficult to find a way out of fear and negative thoughts. We all experience fear and negative thoughts from time to time, and it can be difficult to move past them. The good news is that no matter what we may be struggling with, God has already provided us with the tools we need to overcome our fears and negative thoughts.

This book provides a self-guided road map for overcoming fear and negative thoughts with biblical examples. It is filled with practical advice and examples from the Bible that can help us to break free from our fears and negative thoughts. Through these examples, we can gain insight into how to stay focused on God's will and trust that He will bring us out of our struggles.

I hope that this book will be a source of encouragement and hope for you as you journey through the process of overcoming fear and negative thoughts. May God bless and guide you as you seek Him and trust in His promises.

Kemi Inegbedion, MSM
Realtor® / Residential & Commercial Development/Construction Management. Georgia USA

Dedication

This book is dedicated to God the Father, God the Son, God the Holy Spirit, and to all those who have supported me in my journey toward overcoming my fear and limiting beliefs.

"I sought the Lord, and He heard me, And delivered me from all my fears."
—Psalm 34:4 (NKJV)

Acknowledgments

I want to acknowledge some people who have made this writing a reality and a dream fulfilled.

My spcial thanks go to my dear sisters Temitope Oladapo, Ogenedaji Mowoe-Oyetundun, Olajumoke Ogunleye, and Uwem Aina for their prayers, support, and belief in my abilities and God's call to this assignment.

I am also grateful to my dear friend Joelene Powell for the times we met to pray, process my thoughts, and edit the contents of the worksheets.

I appreciate my parents Mr. Sunday Oladapo and Mrs. Bosede Oladapo for their love and unending prayers over the years.

My sincere gratitude goes to my dearest uncle Jaiye Oladapo for making the publication of this book a reality.

My special thanks to my children, Tami, Timi, Tife, and Tire, for their understanding, attention as I spoke about this assignment, and nightly prayers toward the success of this book.

Finally, I want to thank my husband, Oriyomi, for his love and support in completing this book.

Contents

Preface		17
Introduction		21
Chapter 1	The Journey Begins	25
Chapter 2	Identifying the Fear	41
Chapter 3	Overcoming Limiting Beliefs	53
Chapter 4	The Power of Meditation	67
Chapter 5	Taking Action	81
Chapter 6	Pulling Out the Weeds	95
Chapter 7	Planting and Nurturing Your Seeds	111
Chapter 8	Speak and Walk in Love	127
Testimonials		151
About The Author		156

Preface

In September 2021, my church family was getting ready to move into the new church building they had just acquired. The dedication ceremony was a few days away, and we were all praying and fasting toward D-Day. I would join the daily prayers at church along with our pastors and other parishioners. It was convenient for me to attend the daily evening prayers because my work location was close to the church premises. I was working as a foster care/intact family mental health therapist, which required some level of traveling within the county. I remember driving from Pekin toward East Peoria, Illinois, on one of those days. I had a message by the late Kenneth E. Hagin playing in my vehicle, and I was praying along with the speaker when I heard "Is this really what you want to do?" I knew this was the voice of the Holy Spirit trying to get my attention. I was tired from all the travels and no longer enjoying my current job. The commute was telling on my health as well. I immediately replied, "No, Lord." With tears in my eyes, as I drove to church for the evening prayers, I asked the Lord for help. I went home after the prayers and told my husband I would leave my current job for something closer to home. After two months, I left for a less stressful job with a minimal commute. I thought that was all the Holy Spirit referred to when He asked me the question on that fateful day.

In December of the same year, I continued praying and seeking God's plans for me in the new year. I spent some time fasting and praying as I prepared for the new year. One of those days, as I was praying with my dear sister Gloria Eliezer on the phone, I heard the Holy Spirit again. This time, it had more of an impression on my heart. He said, "It's time to begin the women's group." Prior to the COVID-19 lockdown, I had led a women's prayer group for about two years. The group became a home fellowship in February 2020, and we had only met weekly for two months before the lockdown. We tried meeting virtually on ZOOM for a few months. We later tried to meet in person after the lockdown, and toward the end of the year, we discontinued the meeting. I prayed about this new assignment and began drawing up the programs for the year 2022.

I was ready to begin the women's group as the new year began. I got the message out with the help and support of my pastor (Basil Erebholo), who worked on my first flyer. We were to meet via teleconference call twice monthly. The first set of meetings went well. While this was going on, I was also getting more training. I joined the 100X Wisdom Challenge by Pedro Adao. I also went through Prayer Academy hosted by Pastor Kola Monehin of New Covenant Assembly, Calgary, Canada. I knew both were relevant to my growth and assignment. I was hungry and eager to grow into this assignment. Within the next couple of months, I held virtual meetings while following the training and support I was receiving from the 100X group.

I was contemplating the next topic for my virtual meeting while praying for the ladies who had faithfully joined the monthly programs in May 2022 when the Holy Spirit gave me the title "Speaking Against Fears." He said it was time for me to teach how I overcame the crippling fears that kept me stuck for years. It would be a 6-week challenge, with us meeting virtually once a week for about an hour and a half. I was excited about this and began putting the process together. My 100X family room members asked me two weeks after I started the challenge if I would make an offer for additional training. I responded that I didn't know but must depend on God to show me the next steps since it was His idea.

Additionally, I had to prayerfully seek Him weekly for what to share. By the end of the fourth week, the instruction came, and the Holy Spirit said, "Convert all the videos to texts and make a training workbook out of it." It was going to be a new pathway for me. I shared this instruction with the participants and, after the 6-week challenge, did as instructed.

I did a second edition of this challenge in the fourth quarter of 2022. By then, I already had a workbook to go with the training. Today, as I sit down typing, I know this wouldn't have been a reality if I lived in fear and limiting beliefs. I invite you to journey with me in these practical steps to overcome your fear and limiting beliefs.

"I sought the Lord, and He heard me, And delivered me from all my fears." —Psalm 34:4 (NKJV)

Introduction

Several years ago, I had so much fear that prevented me from moving forward in the desired things. I lived fearfully for my future, marriage, children, career, and even over my destiny. I had reasons to hold on to these fears because, at that time, those reasons were my reality. At the same time, I didn't know what would become of me. I feared for my children's future. I questioned my parenting style. I felt terrible that I was a lousy wife who didn't know how to sustain her marriage, and I felt stuck in my career. I felt insecure at work and struggled to itemize my accomplishment during any appraisal season. This fear was deeply rooted in me and controlled my attitude and outcome.

In 2007, I decided to further my education and began a master's program. I attended lectures for the first semester, and just before exams started, I left the program. I left the program because of my fear of failing but gave a different excuse that was valid. In 2012, I made a second attempt and applied for another program but abandoned it, just like the first one. I aligned my thoughts with my situation then and believed I wasn't good enough for that program. I saw others as better than I and more capable of achieving better results than I could and used that as an excuse for myself. All of these were affecting my life negatively. Not only was I frustrated with myself, but I was also silently jealous of others' accomplishments. In 2015, while carrying this fear, my company decided to transfer me out of Lagos State, Nigeria, to an onsite location in Rivers State. I was unfamiliar with this location, and to make matters worse, I would be working at a seaport. I tried not to go and gave several reasons why sending me to work in that location was a terrible idea. My excuses were: I was recovering from knee arthroscopy; we recently moved into our new home; my husband was studying outside the country, and my support system as a mother of four children was within my home environment. As far as I was concerned, all these reasons were good enough to discourage my company from transferring me and not being the right person for this official assignment.

When I realized that all effort to change their mind was proving abortive and my prayers for God to change their mind were not happening, I asked the Lord if He wanted me to go. His response was very immediate. First, I had this overwhelming peace as a confirmation to go, and then He gave me scriptures to confirm why I needed to go. He said, "For I know the thoughts that I think toward you, says the Lord, thoughts of peace and not of evil, to give you a future and a hope" (Jeremiah 29:11, NKJV). I responded that I had fears about leaving my extended family, as my husband was out of the country studying. I was worried about finding the right support for myself and our children. Lastly, I feared adjusting to life in the new environment. Again, He responded, "You are too worried about mundane things."

As we communed, I remembered the Bible passage He referenced. "As Jesus and His disciples were on their way, He came to a village where a woman named Martha opened her home to him. She had a sister called Mary, who sat at the Lord's feet listening to what he said. But Martha was distracted by all the preparations that had to be made. She came to Him and asked, 'Lord, don't you care that my sister has left me to do the work by myself? Tell her to help me!' 'Martha, Martha,' the Lord answered, 'you are worried and upset about many things, but few things are needed—or indeed only one. Mary has chosen what is better, and it will not be taken away from her'" (Luke 10:38–42, NKJV).

I continued expressing my fears by telling Him I was afraid to go live in that area. Also, He would have to promise to care for my children and me. He gave me His Word again: "Then Peter answered and said to Him, 'See, we have left all and followed You. Therefore what shall we have?' So Jesus said to them, 'Assuredly I say to you, that in the regeneration, when the Son of Man sits on the throne of His glory, you who have followed Me will also sit on twelve thrones, judging the twelve tribes of Israel. And everyone who has left houses or brothers or sisters or father or mother or wife or children or lands, for My name's sake, shall receive a hundredfold and inherit eternal life. But many who are first will be last, and the last first'"(Matthew 19:27–30, NKJV).

All I needed to hear were those reassuring Words from the Lord. I relaxed and said to Him, "Lord, I will obey You and go, seeing that You have given me Your Words." The next day, I called my superior at work and told them I was ready for the relocation. This move began the journey toward **Speaking Against and Overcoming the Fears and Negative Beliefs** in my life and taking action toward fulfilling my God-given assignment and destiny. Just like He told me on that fateful day at about 5 a.m. that His thoughts toward me are good, I believe it's the same for you too.

Do you feel stuck and unfulfilled? Or are you weighed down with so many negative beliefs and fears that have crippled your journey in life? I encourage you not to stop reading this book. Join me as I show you the practical steps the Holy Spirit took me through to overcome these obstacles. They will help you overcome fears that have kept you stuck in life.

CHAPTER 1

The Journey Begins

My family and I moved to a new environment (Port-Harcourt, Rivers State, Nigeria), and we soon found a good church to attend. At that time, the church we attended, The Kings Assembly, was going through a series on Overcoming Fears. I decided to purchase the messages on CDs to listen to again. I knew I had to do something since the fears affected my life and relationships. At this time, I felt so small in my eyes, sought validation from family and friends, and struggled with my self-esteem and self-worth. I remember coming home from work one evening and saying, "The Lord gave me scriptures that convinced me to come to this location. I'm going to look for scriptures that speak about fears. I will write them down, personalize them, and confess them until I have victory over all these fears in my life."

I picked up my Bible, and the first scripture I saw was "I sought the Lord, and He heard me, And delivered me from all my fears" (Psalm 34:4, NKJV). I wrote a personalized statement from the scripture for my daily confession. I even told myself that "all I need is to take all these fears to the Lord in prayers, and He will answer me by freeing me from all of them because His Words and promises cannot lie or fail."

I located a few other scriptures:

> *"So do not fear, for I am with you; do not be dismayed, for I am your God. I will strengthen you and help you; I will uphold you with my righteous right hand." —Isaiah 41:10 (NKJV)*
>
> *"There is no fear in love. But perfect love drives out fear because fear has to do with punishment. The one who fears is not made perfect in love." —1 John 4:18 (NKJV)*
>
> *"For God has not given us a spirit of fear, but of power and love and of a sound mind." —2 Timothy 1:7 (NKJV)*
>
> *"So we may boldly say: 'The Lord is my helper; I will not fear. What can man do to me?'" —Hebrews 13:6; Psalm 118:6 (KJV)*

After locating these Bible passages, I was no longer happy and comfortable with my situation. I knew that change needed to take place in my life. I began to seek the face of the Lord in prayers and use my personalized statements to make daily confessions. I became very intentional about speaking them over my life day and night.

According to the Oxford Online Dictionary, fear is "an unpleasant emotion caused by the belief that someone or something terrible or dangerous will happen. It is an unpleasant emotion resulting from one's beliefs about oneself, someone else, or a life situation." I realized that I believed so many lies about myself. My unpleasant thoughts and negative beliefs about myself impacted my feelings and actions. I couldn't imagine myself doing all that I'm capable of doing today. I thought and affirmed the enemy's lies for a very long time. I saw only the limitations in my situation and, because of my negative thoughts and beliefs, validated them. I believed in a worse outcome and cringed at any opportunity to step forward.

I was not only fearful but also anxious. The Oxford Online Dictionary defines anxiety as "a feeling of worry, or nervousness about an imminent event, or uncertain outcome." I had been a champion at worrying. I stayed up all night brooding and thinking. I spent some nights in tears and lamentation over my life, marriage, children, career, and future. I knew there was more to my life and destiny, but I felt incapable of achieving my goals. After locating those scriptures and writing them down, I began to speak them over my life daily. I confessed what I had written down in the morning as I left for work and returned home. It was easy to do this because I joined my company staff bus to work and back. I made these personalized confessions on weekends as part of my morning devotion and night prayers.

After a while, I started to notice some changes in my life. I began to get a clearer picture of who I am in Christ. This knowledge increased my boldness toward speaking against those crippling fears. The journey that brought me to this position in life began from that point. I'm far from where I started years ago, as I have taken many strides forward.

Why do we have to speak against fear? Whatever we accept is automatically permitted. We sometimes allow negative things to continue in our lives because we have not developed the capacity to reject them or are ignorant of what to do. We speak against fear because:

- It is not from God - "For God has not given us a spirit of fear, but of power and of love and of a sound mind" (2 Timothy 1:7, NKJV). This kind of fear that cripples our ability to achieve goals and move forward in our destiny doesn't come from God.

- It torments - causes mental and physical suffering.

- It deprives one of joy and peace. As living proof, I lacked joy and peace for several years, as I permitted myself to be controlled by fear.

- It distorts one's ability to love - "There is no fear in love. But perfect love drives out fear because fear has to do with punishment. The one who fears is not made perfect in love" (1 John 4:18, NKJV). When you live in fear, to love either yourself or others genuinely becomes a difficult task, as you will continue to look down on yourself and your abilities while thinking of others as better than you. Fear can often lead to feelings of jealousy and resentment toward others as well.

- It deprives one of actualizing their full potential.

In this book, you will identify those fears and negative beliefs in your life, no matter how little or insignificant they may be. It will guide you through steps from Identification of those fears to living a life of fulfillment. There were questions that I had to utilize to discover the specific fear and limiting beliefs that were hindrances in my life. Such questions included:

What is the fear I am currently experiencing?

What does the Word of God say concerning this particular fear?

What is the promise of God concerning this fear, and have I located it in the Bible?

What is God saying to me at this moment concerning the situation?

Have I located the promise? Does the Word of God agree with my current beliefs, thoughts, and emotions about the situation?

What does the word say if the Word of God disagrees with it? And how does the word say I should handle it?

In responding to these questions, I found Psalm 34:4 (NKJV), which says: "For I sought the Lord, and he heard me, and delivered me from all my fears." This version says, 'I sought the Lord.' To seek the Lord is like searching for a thing that is lost. I had lost my peace and joy, among other things, and needed God's intervention. As I continued to search the scriptures, I located 2 Timothy 1:7 (NKJV), which says, "For God has not given us the spirit of fear, but of love, of power, and of a sound mind." I discovered that when there is fear in my life, I am depriving myself of actualizing God's desire for me. Fear and timidity made it difficult for me to walk in power, love, and sound mind.

As a child of God, you are depriving yourself of the perfect love of God, power, and sound mind when you have fear operating in you.

I continued my search because I felt there were more instructions in the Word of God for me. I located a third scripture, 1 John 4:18 (NKJV), "there is no fear in love, but perfect love casts out fear because fear involves torment. But he who fears has not been made perfect in love." Fear and anxiety involve torment, and those were my experience. Lastly, I located Isaiah 41:10, "Fear not for I am with you, Be not dismayed for I am your God, I will strengthen you. Yes, I will help you. I will uphold you with my righteous, right hand." These are God's promises to us, His children. I took these scriptures and declared them over my life and situation. I believed and aligned myself with God's promises for my life.

As highlighted above, we can see that God's promise to His children is not to live in fear. Fear is not from God because it never came from Him. As a mental health therapist by profession, I often say to my clients that fear is an emotional reaction to a situation with a belief in a terrible outcome. This emotional reaction can cause destabilization in the life of the person. God's desire is not to bring destabilization to our lives but promised peace and hope as stated: "For I know the thoughts that I think toward you, says the Lord, thoughts of peace and not of evil, to give you a future and a hope" (Jeremiah 29:11, NKJV). Furthermore, Jesus said to us, "Peace I leave with you, My peace I give to you; not as the world gives do I give to you. Let not your heart be troubled, neither let it be afraid" (John 14:27, NKJV). Therefore, it is the will of God for us not to be troubled but to enjoy peace.

Torment is severe mental and physical suffering, according to the Oxford Online Dictionary. When a person is living under torment, it saps the victim's energy and puts a lot of stress on their body and mind. It affects the person's ability to function effectively, depriving the person of joy, peace, and capacity to love. According to 1 John 4:18 (NKJV), "There is no fear in love. But perfect love drives out fear because fear has to do with punishment. The one who fears is not made perfect in love." Fear and love cannot coexist. As children of God, when we find ourselves acting in fear, we must ask quickly, "Am I walking in love?"

Fear also deprives one of the ability to express their full potential and accomplish things because of all the deprivation that comes with it. He tells us not to be afraid of doing what He's called us to because He promises He is always with us. "The Lord is my helper; I will not fear. What can man do to me?" (Hebrews 13:6; Psalm 118:6, KJV).

You may ask, "How do I begin to speak against the fear in my life?"

I have taken the time to write my journey and process in this book. My goal is to guide you through the steps I took as led by the Holy Spirit to overcome the fears in my life. This practical tool is not meant to be used once but continually in our daily life as we come in contact with varying degrees of fear. I know this because:

God is deeply interested in your well-being and will answer you when you call upon Him

In Luke 18:1-6, Jesus spoke about the importunate widow and, in His illustration, explained how we ought to pray and not faint. In this passage, the widow kept demanding justice from the unrighteous judge until she received her request. He further stated that if this unrighteous judge could do that for the widow, God would grant the request of His chosen people quicker than that.

"Then He spoke a parable to them, that men always ought to pray and not lose heart, saying: 'There was in a certain city a judge who did not fear God nor regard man. Now there was a widow in that city, and she came to him, saying, "Get justice for me from my adversary." And he would not for a while; but afterward he said within himself, "Though I do not fear God nor regard man, yet because this widow troubles me I will avenge her, lest by her continual coming she weary me."' Then the Lord said, 'Hear what the unjust Judge said. And shall God not avenge His own elect who cry out day and night to Him, though He bears long with them? I tell you that He will avenge them speedily. Nevertheless, when the Son of Man comes, will He really find faith on the earth?'" (Luke 18:1-8 NKJV).

This widow appealed to the judge. Similarly, God wants us to speak to Him when we experience challenging situations.

> *"Hear my cry, O God; Attend to my prayer. From the end of the earth I will cry to You, When my heart is overwhelmed; Lead me to the rock that is higher than I."*

—*Psalm 61:1-2 (NKJV)*

"I sought the Lord, and He heard me, And delivered me from all my fears." —Psalm 34:4 (NKJV)

When you are overwhelmed with life situations, I encourage you to seek the Lord and speak against your fears.

God wants you to speak against the situation and not to align with it in your confessions

The Israelite army was terrified by the Philistines for 40 days. The captain of their army, Goliath, tormented them, and King Saul couldn't face him on the battlefield until David showed up at the scene. David spoke directly to Goliath, telling him that God would deliver him and give victory to his army. In this situation, Goliath represents a fearful situation for the military of Israel. Still, he was defeated because David spoke against him and took the necessary action to defeat him. He went after him, just like he did to the bear and lion that came after his sheep.

"But David said to Saul, 'Your servant used to keep his father's sheep, and when a lion or a bear came and took a lamb out of the flock, I went out after it and struck it, and delivered the lamb from its mouth; and when it arose against me, I caught it by its beard, and struck and killed it. Your servant has killed both lion and bear, and this uncircumcised Philistine will be like one of them, seeing he has defied the armies of the living God.' Moreover, David said, 'The Lord, who delivered me from the paw of the lion and from the paw of the bear, He will deliver me from the hand of this Philistine'" (1 Samuel 17:34-37, NKJV).

Fears are like mountains, obstacles, and limitations that prevent one from moving forward or even getting to their desired destination. Jesus also instructed us to speak to them, and they will obey.

"So Jesus answered and said to them, Have faith in God. For assuredly, I say to you, whoever says to this mountain, 'Be removed and be cast into the sea,' and does not doubt in his heart but believes that those things he says will be done, he will have whatever he says. Therefore I say to you, whatever things you ask when you pray, believe that you receive them, and you will have them" (Mark 11:22–24, NKJV).

He desires for you to meditate on the Word of God

Robert J. Morgan stated in his book *100 Bible Verses* that the instruction given to Joshua to meditate on the law in the Bible verse Joshua 1:8 was threefold, implying to memorize, visualize, and personalize the promises of God for you. These were the same strategies that I utilized. It is affirming the promises of God and laying hold of them. It helps you shift your focus from crippling fear to the solution available. It facilitates the assurance of victory. Just before the children of Israel conquered the land of Jericho, the Lord told Joshua that he had already given them the land of Jericho.

> *"And the Lord said to Joshua: See! I have given Jericho into your hand, its king, and the mighty men of valor." —Joshua 6:2 (NKJV)*

Before this encounter, the Lord had told Joshua that he would lead the Israelites to take possession of the land of Canaan and commanded him to keep His laws and meditate upon them because his success in this assignment depended on them. "This Book of the Law shall not depart from your mouth, but you shall meditate on it day and night, that you may observe to do according to all that is written in it. For then you will make your way prosperous, and then you will have good success" (Joshua 1:8, NKJV). You must be able to see the success that God has given to you, and in other to see it, you must meditate upon the promises of God for you in that area of your life. Speak the promises of God back to yourself. When you meditate on the promises of God, these promises become magnified in your mind, causing the fears to diminish. Once magnified, you will begin to take bold steps based on the promises of God.

God desires you not to give up until the desired change becomes a reality

Many times we give up too soon. We make statements like, "Oh, I prayed in the morning. I prayed yesterday about it, and that is enough." Remember the story of that persistent widow in Luke 18. She was used as an illustration by Jesus Christ on why we shouldn't give up until the change we so desire becomes a reality. She kept returning to the judge until he avenged her of her adversary. Fear is our adversary, and until we are avenged, we shouldn't give up speaking against it. Additionally, in the story of the prophet Elijah, God promised to send rain upon the land after a period of famine. "And it came to pass after many days that the word of the Lord came to Elijah, in the third year, saying, Go, present yourself to Ahab, and I will send rain on the earth" (1 Kings 18:1, NKJV). Elijah took this promise and began to pray for rain. What was in the land was famine, but he prayed earnestly for the rain to become a reality and didn't stop praying until the rain fell.

"Then Elijah said to Ahab, 'Go up, eat and drink; for there is the sound of abundance of rain.' So Ahab went up to eat and drink. And Elijah went up to the top of Carmel; then he bowed down on the ground, put his face between his knees, and said to his servant, 'Go up now, look toward the sea.' So he went up and looked, and said, 'There is nothing.' And seven times he said, 'Go again.' Then it came to pass the seventh time, that he said, 'There is a cloud, as small as a man's hand, rising out of the sea!' So he said, 'Go up, say to Ahab, Prepare your chariot, and go down before the rain stops you.' Now it happened in the meantime that the sky became black with clouds and wind, and there was a heavy rain. So Ahab rode away and went to Jezreel. Then the hand of the Lord came upon Elijah; and he girded up his loins and ran ahead of Ahab to the entrance of Jezreel" (1 Kings 18:41–46, NKJV). This same encounter was referenced in the New Testament as an illustration to pray until the desired result is achieved. "Elijah was a man with a nature like ours, and he prayed earnestly that it would not rain; and it did not rain on the land for three years and six months. And he prayed again, and the heaven gave rain, and the earth produced its fruit" (James 5:17–18, NKJV).

I look at my life today, and I'm full of joy for answered prayers over many years of praying for different areas of my life. I have kept at it, and there are still some that I have continued to pray about until I see their manifestation. One such prayer is to share this success nugget with several people going through fears and guide them in the path, just as the Holy Spirit showed me. My desire for you is that you will keep on asking and not give up hope until your joy is complete. "Until now you have not asked [the Father] for anything in My name; but now ask and keep on asking and you will receive, so that your joy may be full and complete" (John 16:24, AMP).

Above all, God wants you to have the attitude of thanksgiving

Giving thanks is our password to unlocking the mysteries of God for us. God wants us to approach Him with a grateful heart, knowing He will grant our desires. God dwells in our praises. "But you are holy, Enthroned in the praises of Israel" (Psalm 22:3, NKJV).

Our praises are like sweet incense before God. When we praise God, we give him a sweet sacrifice that has a pleasing aroma. God wants to be full of it. "May my prayer be set before you like incense; may the lifting up of my hands be like the evening sacrifice" (Psalm 141:2, NKJV).

The story of King Jehoshaphat and the children of Judah in 2 Chronicles 20 is a good illustration of overcoming situational fear using the power of praise and worship to God. They faced three great opposing armies that threatened to invade and take over their land. The king and the people of the land cried unto the Lord in their moment of distress and fear. The Lord gave them a strategy that involved them praising God. On the day of battle, they only needed to praise while God fought for them and defeated their enemies.

"So they rose early in the morning and went out into the

Wilderness of Tekoa; and as they went out, Jehoshaphat stood and said, Hear me, O Judah and you inhabitants of Jerusalem: Believe in the Lord your God, and you shall be established; believe His prophets, and you shall prosper. And when he had consulted with the people, he appointed those who should sing to the Lord, and who should praise the beauty of holiness, as they went out before the army and were saying: Praise the Lord, For His mercy endures forever. Now when they began to sing and to praise, the Lord set ambushes against the people of Ammon, Moab, and Mount Seir, who had come against Judah; and they were defeated. For the people of Ammon and Moab stood up against the inhabitants of Mount Seir to utterly kill and destroy them. And when they had made an end of the inhabitants of Seir, they helped to destroy one another" (2 Chronicles 20:20–23, NKJV).

I was so disturbed about the conclusion of my academics during the COVID-19 lockdown. At this time, we had almost exhausted all our savings on my master's program, and I feared that we would not be able to get enough money for me to complete my program. While praying and praising God for how far He's helped me, He gave me a strategy on what to do. I quickly contacted my school registrar to see if it was possible for me to complete my program earlier than scheduled. He said it was possible as long as I could get a place to do part of my internship since I would need to achieve certain hours for graduation. I had two weeks to get all these arrangements worked out, but I knew it would work out since it was God's leading. I contacted my academic advisor, who gave me names of places to contact and said the time was short but I should contact them. Within two days, I got a positive response from one. He accepted my application to do part of my internship with his college.

As I was nearing the end of my internship, there was a spike in the rate of college students contracting the COVID-19 virus on campus, and the school had to close. I was short on my hours, and it seemed like I wouldn't graduate that semester. I became fearful again. The enemy began to project another fear on me. I remember one of those nights when I stayed up so worried that I felt I would choke. I remember calling my dear friend Uwem Aina to tell her what was happening to me. She said, "Lola, you've passed through worse situations, and just as God came through for you, He will do it again." She also said, "You know what to do." Indeed, I knew what to do.

When I returned home that night, I prayed with my family, and as soon as everyone was in bed, I began to praise God. I praised and danced from around 11 p.m. till about 1 a.m. After my praise dance, I began to laugh at the enemy. I said to him, "Victory is mine in Jesus' name. Amen." When I got to my campus the next day, my advisor said that I shouldn't worry about my graduation because they would make an exception for me due to the pandemic, and I would be graduating as expected. When you turn to thanksgiving, God's mighty and miraculous hands begin to act on your behalf. He did it for Jehoshaphat and the children of Judah. He also showed up for me in my testimonies above. God is more than able to meet you at that very point of your need. That is why we are encouraged to pray and give thanks to God. "Be anxious for nothing, but in everything by prayer and supplication, with thanksgiving, let your requests be made known to God; and the peace of God, which surpasses all understanding, will guard your hearts and minds through Christ Jesus" (Philippians 4:6-7, NKJV).

What outcome will you expect from following this process?

As we journey through this process, below are the expected outcomes:

- You will learn to identify each fear and the promises of God that are contrary to the fear(s).

- You will understand and begin to overcome the limiting beliefs associated with the fears.

- You will gain clarity in understanding the promises of God and take appropriate actions toward your desires and goals in life.

- As you replace those fears with the promises of God, you will develop a renewed love and a deeper level of intimacy with the Holy Spirit as you speak and affirm them..

- You will develop the boldness to take the necessary steps toward actualizing your kingdom assignment and goals.

- You will learn to identify and uproot anything contrary to your desired outcome as directed by the Holy Spirit. Such things are known as weeds.

God's desire is for you to fulfill your purpose and not be overtaken by fears and limiting beliefs. So, I encourage you to join me on this journey today as I take you through overcoming the fears and limiting beliefs in your life.

CHAPTER 2

Identifying the Fear

The first step on this journey is to identify the fear(s) and list them. The workbook contains worksheets for each chapter as a guide to making a list. As mentioned earlier, I had fears over my marriage, career, and children. I had first to identify what they were.

Once you have made a list of the fears, you will look through the Bible for scriptures that speak against them or tell you what to do when experiencing them. Remember that the Bible is God speaking to you. It is our instruction manual and spiritual guide as children of God. We are to live by the Word of God.

> *"So He humbled you, allowed you to hunger, and fed you with manna which you did not know nor did your fathers know, that He might make you know that man shall not live by bread alone; but man lives by every word that proceeds from the mouth of the Lord." —Deuteronomy 8:3 (NKJV)*

> *"But He answered and said, It is written, 'Man shall not live by bread alone, but by every word that proceeds from the mouth of God.'"* —Matthew 4:4 (NKJV)

You need to identify these scriptures to know the promises of God for you. Many children of God are ignorant of the promises of God for them. As a result, the enemy takes advantage of their ignorance. When you know God's provision for you, you will take advantage of it because it is your heritage.

> *"My people are destroyed for lack of knowledge. Because you have rejected knowledge, I also will reject you from being priest for Me; Because you have forgotten the law of your God, I also will forget your children."* —Hosea 4:6 (NKJV)

The enemy plans to take advantage of the believer, and one of his weapons is ignorance. Getting into the Word of God to know the promises that are freely given to us gives us joy, victory, and success over the schemes of the enemy.

> *"When I discovered your words, I devoured them. They are my joy and my heart's delight, for I bear your name, O Lord God of Heaven's Armies."* —Jeremiah 15:16 (NLT)

> *"This Book of the Law shall not depart from your mouth, but you shall meditate in it day and night, that you may observe to do according to all that is written in it. For then you will make your way prosperous, and then you will have good success."* —Joshua 1:8 (NKJV)

Please use Bible translations that would be easy for you to understand.

Once you have written down the scriptures, you must meditate on them. According to Strong's Concordance, the word 'meditate' in Hebrew means 'hagah,' which means to "murmur, mutter, speak, utter it, muse." When you meditate on these scriptures, you affirm them to yourself by memorizing, visualizing, and personalizing them. In-depth explanation on the Power of Meditation is in chapter 4 of this book.

The Lord told Joshua that he would prosper in his assignment when he meditated on the promises of God as written in the law for him. The task ahead of him was a very great one. Moses had brought the Israelites out of Egypt, but now, Joshua must bring them into the promised land.

> *"This Book of the Law shall not depart from your mouth, but you shall meditate in it day and night, that you may observe to do according to all that is written in it. For then you will make your way prosperous, and then you will have good success." —Joshua 1:8 (NKJV)*

Also, David understood the importance of meditating on the Word of God for his prosperity and victories over his enemies. No wonder he began the book of Psalms with this statement.

> *"Blessed is the man Who walks not in the counsel of the ungodly, Nor stands in the path of sinners, Nor sits in the seat of the scornful; But his delight is in the law of the Lord, And in His law, he meditates day and night. He shall be*

like a tree Planted by the rivers of water, That brings forth its fruit in its season, Whose leaf also shall not wither; And whatever he does shall prosper." —Psalm 1:1–3 (NKJV)

Furthermore, he expressed that this is what he does all day. He didn't carry the Torah with him. Still, he memorized, visualized, and personalized them to the point where he was wholly aligned with them.

"Oh, how I love Your law! It is my meditation all the day." —Psalm 119:97 (NKJV)

As mentioned in the previous chapters, I looked for scriptures that related to my situation in 2016. I took the steps of meditating upon them. Please write a minimum of three for each category you identify. Some of the scriptures may be applicable across different types. In my case, I had one that I located first that applied to all. In addition, I looked for more for each category. Why more than one passage? Remember when Satan tried to tempt Jesus? He didn't leave Jesus after the first attempt. He tempted Jesus Christ three times. I'm not making this a principle. It's just to let you know that having more than one makes you grounded against Satan's schemes.

Identifying Fear

List the top 5 to 10 areas of your life where you are experiencing fear (e.g., family, relationship, marriage, career, future, children, health, etc.):

_____

_____

_____

_____

_____

_____

_____

_____

_____

_____

Locating the Promise

Write two scriptures that are connected to your fears. (Example: "I sought the Lord, and He heard me, And delivered me from all my fears." —Psalm 34:4, NKJV)

Scripture 1:

Scripture 2:

Locating the Promise

In addition to the two scriptures you wrote above, locate and write three scriptures connected to the areas of your life where you are experiencing fear that you listed. Make sure to write at least three for each category. Example: My Future — "For I know the plans I have for you, says the Lord. They are plans for good and not for disaster, to give you a future and hope" (Jeremiah 29:11, NLT).

Scripture 1:

Scripture 2:

Scripture 3:

My Notes

CHAPTER 3

Overcoming Limiting Beliefs

The Oxford Online Dictionary states that fear is an "unpleasant emotion caused by the belief that something terrible or dangerous will happen." It believes the worst outcome. Fear is like an expression of something that is deep. So, it's a product of what we believe. "To believe something is to accept that the thing is true, it is real, and it exists" (Online Dictionary). To overcome the fear, you want to identify the cause(s) of the fear. Fear doesn't happen in isolation; a belief about yourself, your situation, or the world perpetuates it. Belief is at the root of fear. Despite witnessing their great deliverance from bondage in the land of Egypt, the children of Israel continued to live in fear in the wilderness because of their beliefs. Ten out of the twelve leaders sent to spy on the land of Canaan came back with a negative and fearful report.

A limiting belief is a state of mind about oneself that shrinks one's capacity to do a thing. It is a mindset that restricts you from achieving your goals and attaining your full potentials in life. This mindset limited Israel's ability to "see" the vision of God for them concerning their goal – Canaan.

"Now they departed and returned to Moses and Aaron and all the congregation of the children of Israel in the Wilderness of Paran, at Kadesh; they brought back word to them and all the congregation and showed them the fruit of the land. Then they told him and said: 'We went to the land where you sent us. It truly flows with milk and honey, and this is its fruit. Nevertheless, the people who dwell in the land are strong; the cities are fortified and very large; moreover, we saw the descendants of Anak there. The Amalekites dwell in the land of the South; the Hittites, the Jebusites, and the Amorites dwell in the mountains; and the Canaanites dwell by the sea and along the banks of the Jordan.' Then Caleb quieted the people before Moses and said, 'Let us go up at once and take possession, for we are well able to overcome it.' But the men who had gone up with him said, 'We are not able to go up against the people, for they are stronger than we.' And they gave the children of Israel a bad report of the land which they had spied out, saying, 'The land through which we have gone as spies is a land that devours its inhabitants, and all the people whom we saw in it are men of great stature. There we saw the giants (the descendants of Anak came from the giants), and we were like grasshoppers in our own sight, and so we were in their sight'" (Numbers 13:26-33, NKJV).

These ten leaders chose to focus on the negative and dismissed the fertility of the land. The Israelites quickly forgot every miraculous act of God in the wilderness. They continued to provoke God in their reactions toward any difficulty faced on the journey. We are warned not to be like them because their unbeliefs prevented them from entering the promised land. God referred to them as stiffnecked people.

"Therefore, as the Holy Spirit says: 'Today, if you will hear His voice, Do not harden your hearts as in the rebellion, In the day of trial in the wilderness, Where your fathers tested Me, tried Me, And saw My works forty years. Therefore I was angry with that generation, And said, "They always go astray in their heart, And they have not known My ways." So I swore in My wrath, "They shall not enter My rest."' Beware, brethren, lest there be in any of you an evil heart of unbelief in departing from the living God; but exhort one another daily, while it is called 'Today,' lest any of you be hardened through the deceitfulness of sin. For we have become partakers of Christ if we hold the beginning of our confidence steadfast to the end, while it is said: 'Today if you will hear His voice, Do not harden your hearts as in the rebellion. For who, having heard, rebelled? Indeed, was it not all who came out of Egypt, led by Moses? Now with whom was He angry forty years? Was it not with those who sinned, whose corpses fell in the wilderness? And to whom did He swear that they would not enter His rest, but to those who did not obey? So we see that they could not enter in because of unbelief.'" —(Hebrews 3:7–19, NKJV)

"Furthermore, the LORD spake unto me, saying, I have seen this people, and, behold, it is a stiffnecked people" — Deuteronomy 9:13 (KJV)

One can ask why it was so difficult for the Israelites to believe in God. They had all through their lives known slavery and hardship. They were already conditioned to this life of bondage in Egypt. The later part of their time in Egypt was full of bitter experiences following the enthronement of a pharaoh that didn't know Joseph. So, physically, they left Egypt, but mentally, they remained in bondage. This belief in the worst outcome blinded their minds from believing in God's mighty power and acts. They couldn't see the best result. They couldn't see beyond the time that they spent in Egypt. They believed and accepted that their outcome of bondage was accurate and true. It was going to happen even in the wilderness.

"Now a new king over Egypt arose who did not know Joseph. And he said to his people, 'Look, the people of the children of Israel are more and mightier than we; come, let us deal shrewdly with them, lest they multiply, and it happens, in the event of war, that they also join our enemies and fight against us, and so go up out of the land.' Therefore they set taskmasters over them to afflict them with their burdens. And they built for Pharaoh supply cities, Pithom and Raamses." —Exodus 1:8–11 (NKJV)

To identify these limiting beliefs, you will need to answer questions that will help you dig into the root of the fears, such as finding out the situations of your life, history, significant events, or circumstances that have brought you to the point where you have become so fearful. It could be due to issues in your family of origin, adverse childhood experiences, financial hardship, delayed or truncated career, marital crises, or parenting keeping your focus on the worst outcome, just like the Israelites in the wilderness.

To overcome these negative beliefs, we must first identify them and find the promises of God that speak against the beliefs in the scriptures. The Lord promised Abraham that his descendants would be in Egypt for 400 years, but He will bring them out with a mighty hand.

> *"As the sun was going down, Abram fell into a deep sleep, and a terrifying darkness came down over him. Then the Lord said to Abram, 'You can be sure that your descendants will be strangers in a foreign land, where they will be oppressed as slaves for 400 years. But I will punish the nation that enslaves them, and in the end they will come away with great wealth. (As for you, you will die in peace and be buried at a ripe old age.) After four generations your descendants will return here to this land, for the sins of the Amorites do not yet warrant their destruction.'"* — *Genesis 15:12–16 (NLT)*

God promised the descendants of Abraham deliverance. He promised to give them the land. He wouldn't keep them in the wilderness because He had an excellent destination for them.

> *"Now go and call together all the elders of Israel. Tell them, 'Yahweh, the God of your ancestors—the God of Abraham, Isaac, and Jacob—has appeared to me. He told me, 'I have been watching closely, and I see how the Egyptians are treating you. I have promised to rescue you from your oppression in Egypt. I will lead you to a land flowing with milk and honey—the land where the Canaanites, Hittites, Amorites, Perizzites, Hivites, and Jebusites now live.'"* — *Exodus 3:16–17 (NLT)*

We overcome these negative and limiting beliefs with the Word of God. Believing comes from the heart, and there is a connection between what we speak and believe. We have to assess if our beliefs align with them to speak effectively against fears, just as we started doing in the previous chapter. In other words, your beliefs must match up with the scriptures and your confessions. God looks at the heart, and He searches the thoughts and intents of your heart to know if they are in sync with your confessions. When choosing the next king to take over from king Saul, the prophet Samuel was looking at the physical appearance of the sons of Jesse, but God told him, "I look at the heart." He knew who believed in Him or not through their heart.

> *"But the Lord said to Samuel, 'Don't judge by his appearance or height, for I have rejected him. The Lord doesn't see things the way you see them. People judge by outward appearance, but the Lord looks at the heart.'" —1 Samuel 16:7 (NLT)*

God called David a man after His heart.

> *"And when He had removed him, He raised up for them David as king, to whom also He gave testimony and said, 'I have found David the son of Jesse, a man after My own heart, who will do all My will.'" —Acts 13:22 (NJKV)*

He doesn't just want us to come near Him with our lips or speak when our hearts are far from him. When we do so, we are not different from the Israelites in the wilderness who lived in unbelief and the Pharisees and Scribes whom Jesus referred to as hypocrites.

> *"These people draw near to Me with their mouth, And honor Me with their lips, But their heart is far from Me." — Matthew 15:8 (NKJV)*

He wants us to believe His promises for us. When we do so, our speaking is effective, and we will receive from Him.

> *"So Jesus answered and said to them, 'Have faith in God. For assuredly, I say to you, whoever says to this mountain, "Be removed and be cast into the sea," and does not doubt in his heart but believes that those things he says will be done, he will have whatever he says. Therefore I say to you, whatever things you ask when you pray, believe that you receive them, and you will have them.'" —Mark 11:22-24 (NKJV)*

When you believe in the promises of God and speak them as commanded, you will overcome the limiting beliefs and begin to walk in victory and success. The Word of God displaces those fears and limiting beliefs and gives you a new perspective on your life based on his desires for you and your destiny.

The Root of Fear

Fear is an unpleasant emotion caused by the belief that something terrible or dangerous will happen. It is believing in the worst outcome.

Every expression of fear has a cause, whether past, present, or future, but mainly caused by history, past events, situations, or circumstances.

Make a list of the cause or causes of the fears you listed above. Example: "Fear - Future"; "Cause - Past failures."

_____

_____

_____

_____

_____

_____

_____

Identify Limiting Beliefs

Fears are products of limiting beliefs - to accept that something is true, real, or exists based on your perception of life and experiences. What are your beliefs about the cause(s) of your fears? What lie or lies from the enemy have you been believing and continue to hold onto as a reality?

No	Cause	Belief(s)
1	*Example: Future*	*I have failed several times and don't believe that my life will ever have the right outcome.*

No	Cause	Belief(s)

Locating God's Promises

Write two scriptures that speak directly to your belief in God's promises. Example: **Future** - "For the lovers of God may suffer adversity and stumble seven times, but they will continue to rise over and over again." —Proverbs 24:16a (TPT)

Belief(s)	Scripture(s)

Belief(s)	Scripture(s)

My Notes

CHAPTER 4

The Power of Meditation

In this chapter, we will be looking at understanding the power of meditation. As defined in the previous chapter, the word 'meditate' in Hebrew means 'hagah,' which means to "murmur, mutter, speak, utter it, and muse." When you meditate on the Word of God, following its meaning in Hebrew, you will be speaking it back to yourself. So, the question remains "Why is meditating on the Word of God good for you to overcome fear and limiting beliefs?" In the book of Joshua, God gave Joshua, who was now to assume the role of the leader of Israelites after his master Moses' death, instructions concerning his success in leading the people into the promised land.

> *"After the death of Moses, the servant of the Lord, it came to pass that the Lord spoke to Joshua the son of Nun, Moses' assistant, saying: 'Moses, My servant is dead. Now therefore, arise, go over this Jordan, you and all this people, to the land which I am giving to them—the children of Israel. Every place that the sole of your foot will tread upon I have given you, as I said to Moses. From the wilderness*

and this Lebanon as far as the great river, the River Euphrates, all the land of the Hittites, and to the Great Sea toward the going down of the sun shall be your territory. No man shall be able to stand before you all the days of your life; as I was with Moses, I will be with you. I will not leave you nor forsake you. Be strong and of good courage, for to this people you shall divide as an inheritance the land which I swore to their fathers to give them. Only be strong and very courageous, that you may observe to do according to all the law which Moses, My servant commanded you; do not turn from it to the right hand or to the left, that you may prosper wherever you go. This Book of the Law shall not depart from your mouth, but you shall meditate in it day and night, that you may observe to do according to all that is written in it. For then you will make your way prosperous, and then you will have good success." —*Joshua 1:1-8 (NKJV)*

Joshua had been with Moses all through the years in the wilderness. He experienced all the negative behaviors and attitudes of the children of Israel, their stubbornness, murmurings, and disobedience toward Moses and God. He is now receiving the instruction to lead them into the promised land. In verse 8 of the above chapter, God gives him specific instructions for his success in this assignment.

"This Book of the Law shall not depart from your mouth, but you shall meditate in it day and night, that you may observe to do according to all that is written in it. For then you will make your way prosperous, and then you will have good success." —*Joshua 1:8 (NKJV)*

Robert J. Morgan stated in his book *100 Bible Verses* that this instruction contains a three-fold command. First, "not to depart from your mouth" means you are speaking, reading, repeating it and hearing it to yourself. Secondly, to "meditate on it day or night" means to visualize, ponder over, and chew the Word and let it digest into your system. In other words, see yourself as one with the Word by personalizing it. Being one with the Word was also understood by Jeremiah when he said in the passage below:

> *"Thy words were found, and I did eat them, and thy word was unto me the joy and rejoicing of mine heart: for I am called by thy name, O Lord God of hosts." —Jeremiah 15:16 (KJV)*

Lastly, the Lord said, "... that you may observe to do according to all that is written in it," meaning you have to put it into practice and take action based on the Word of God.

I would explain the three S's in this passage that make meditation powerful. The first S is **Speak.** The phrase "Let it not depart from your mouth" means speak or say it. You cannot be silent and continue to accommodate the fear. You have to begin to speak and affirm the promises of God over your life. When saying the Word of God, you are kick-starting a change process. This transformation can only occur when you have continuously repeated the Word of God to yourself. As you repeat the Word, you hear it, and you begin to see yourself as capable of doing what the Word says you can do.

> *"So then faith cometh by hearing and hearing by the word of God." —Romans 10:17 (KJV)*

Therefore, we hear by speaking and repeating the promises of God to ourselves. As you say these promises continuously to yourself, they become louder than the voice of fears and limiting beliefs. According to neuroscience, words we hear repeatedly go right into our subconscious mind and begin to affect our behaviors and response to situations. Until I started speaking the promises of God to myself, I believed the enemy's lie. I believed all the whispers and negative words the enemy gave me. I lived in fear and was limited because they affected my response to life. The Word of God is powerful, and when we speak them, power is released. As you continue to speak the promises of God, they become magnified in your mind, and the negative voices get minimized.

The second S is to **See,** which implies the power of vision. Your ability to visualize and have a mental image of what you desire. The Bible tells us the story of a woman who had suffered a hemorrhage for twelve years. She was desperate for her healing. That woman visualized herself getting up from her sick bed at home, walking toward Jesus, and pushing through the crowd to get her miracle. First, she spoke to herself about what she desired.

> *"And behold, a woman who had suffered from a flow of blood for twelve years came up behind Him and touched the fringe of His garment; For she kept saying to herself, If I only touch His garment, I shall be restored to health. Jesus turned around and, seeing her, He said, Take courage, daughter! Your faith has made you well. And at once the woman was restored to health." —Matthew 9:20–22 (AMPC)*

In helping Abraham to visualize how numerous his descendants would be on earth, God introduced this principle to him. First, by changing his name from 'Abram,' meaning exalted father, to 'Abraham,' meaning the father of many nations. Imagine Abraham repeating his name to himself and everyone in contact with him. Additionally, God promised him that his descendants would be as numerous as the stars and sand on the seashore.

> *"Nor shall your name any longer be Abram [high, exalted father]; but your name shall be Abraham [father of a multitude], for I have made you the father of many nations."*
> —*Genesis 17:5 (AMPC)*

> *"That in blessing I will bless thee, and in multiplying I will multiply thy seed as the stars of the heaven, and as the sand which is upon the sea shore; and thy seed shall possess the gate of his enemies."* —*Genesis 22:17 (KJV)*

You must also visualize yourself overcoming the fear and stepping into your God-given purpose as you speak.

Lastly, the third S is to **Sink in**. It is letting the Word digest and become part of you. To personalize the promises is to become one with your confession and your affirmations. As the Word of God continues to sink in, it digests and nourishes you, resulting in a desired end.

> "How sweet are thy words unto my taste! yea, sweeter than honey to my mouth." —*Psalm 119:103 (KJV)*

> "When I discovered your words, I devoured them. They

are my joy and my heart's delight, for I bear your name, O Lord God of Heaven's Armies." —Jeremiah 15:16 (NLT)

The power of meditation requires you to speak, see, and allow the Word of God to sink into you. As you continue to engage in them, your boldness to respond based on God's promises becomes magnified.

As a mental health therapist, I often inform my clients of the importance of replacing negative thoughts and words with positive ones. Research has shown that one of the features of mood disorders such as depression and anxiety disorder is a negative thinking pattern which often leads to adverse outcomes. Utilizing meditation with the Word of God is a powerful tool to help promote your mental and emotional well-being as you journey toward actualizing your desires in life.

Personalization of the Promises

> *"This Book of the Law shall not depart from your mouth, but you shall meditate in it day and night, that you may observe to do according to all that is written in it. For then you will make your way prosperous, and then you will have good success."* —Joshua 1:8 (NKJV)

According to Robert J. Morgan, this passage contains a threefold command:

1. Not depart from your mouth - speak it, read it, repeat it, and hear it
2. Meditate on it day and night - memorize it, visualize it, and personalize it
3. Put it into practice and obey it

Using the above command, write a personal statement for each of the five scriptures you wrote in the previous chapters.

Personal Statement 1:

_____

_____

_____

_____

_____

Personal Statement 2:

Personal Statement 3:

Personal Statement 4:

Personal Statement 5:

Set a time

The Lord instructed Joshua to meditate on the book of the law day and night. "This Book of the Law shall not depart from your mouth, but you shall meditate in it day and night, that you may observe to do according to all that is written in it. For then you will make your way prosperous, and then you will have good success." (Joshua 1:8, NKJV) David said that he meditates all day long. "Oh, how I love Your law! It is my meditation all the day." (Psalm 119:97, NKJV) When I began this journey, I would speak and mutter it to myself in the morning and evening.

Choose your time and make it a special time for you and God. Set a reminder for yourself.

My Notes

CHAPTER 5

Taking Action

Taking action is vital to overcoming limitations and obtaining God's promises. In the story of the woman who had suffered from bleeding for 12 years, which was used as an illustration in the previous chapter, we saw that she didn't just speak to herself; she took the necessary action toward her desire.

> *"And there was a woman who had had a flow of blood for twelve years, And who had endured much suffering under [the hands of] many physicians and had spent all that she had, and was no better but instead grew worse. She had heard the reports concerning Jesus, and she came up behind Him in the throng and touched His garment, For she kept saying, If I only touch His garments, I shall be restored to health. And immediately her flow of blood was dried up at the source, and suddenly she felt in her body that she was healed of her distressing ailment." —Mark 5:25-29 (AMPC)*

As you continue to speak against those fears and limiting beliefs, the Words of the Lord begin to magnify in your mind and go into your subconscious mind, causing a reaction and action contrary to what the fears had created in you because they are now minimized. Action-taking helps you to solidify the new experience. Why must you take action? Because even the Bible says that if you have faith without corresponding action, it is dead. Action-taking brings to life your new reality. "So also faith, if it does not have works (deeds and actions of obedience to back it up), by itself is destitute of power (inoperative, dead)" (James 2:17, AMPC). The book of Hebrews chapter eleven is dedicated to men and women who did extraordinary exploits because they all mixed their faith and confessions with corresponding actions.

Remember that the words you have been speaking are God's promises to you. Those words are God speaking directly to you because the Bible contains God's promises and prophesies to us, His Children. God is speaking to you through these daily confessions, declarations, and prayers you have been engaging in over the past few chapters. According to the Bible, God's Words are not just empty promises. His Words always fulfill their purposes because He desires them to accomplish that in our lives.

> *"For as the rain comes down, and the snow from heaven, And do not return there, But water the earth, And make it bring forth and bud, That it may give seed to the sower. And bread to the eater, So shall My word be that goes forth from My mouth; It shall not return to Me void, But it shall accomplish what I please, And it shall prosper in the thing for which I sent it." —Isaiah 55:10–11 (NKJV)*

However, we have a part to play in actualizing God's promises to us. If we truly say we believe what His promises say to us, then we have to do what the Word says to do. If we do not take action, the Word cannot affect us.

> *"But be doers of the word, and not hearers only, deceiving yourselves. For if anyone is a hearer of the word and not a doer, he is like a man observing his natural face in a mirror; for he observes himself, goes away, and immediately forgets what kind of man he was. But he who looks into the perfect law of liberty and continues in it, and is not a forgetful hearer but a doer of the work, this one will be blessed in what he does." —James 1:22-25 (NKJV)*

The woman in the above passage we read did not just think and speak to herself. After speaking, she began to move in the crowd toward Jesus. She didn't stay at home wishing that Jesus would come to meet her where she lived. No, she pushed herself through the crowd to act upon her confessions and received healing.

Another person who took action after speaking in the Bible is David. David got to the camp and heard the captain of the Philistine army bragging. He also saw how fearful King Saul and the army of Israel were. David chose to rescue the Israelites from shame and reproach. He stated precisely what he would do to this uncircumcised Philistine because he had a pedigree of exploits of God's deliverance. David acted swiftly upon his confessions. He didn't say "Let me wait after speaking"; rather, he moved in the direction of his words.

"So the Philistine came, and began drawing near to David, and the man who bore the shield went before him. And when the Philistine looked about and saw David, he disdained[d] him; for he was only a youth, ruddy and good-looking. So the Philistine said to David, 'Am I a dog, that you come to me with sticks?' And the Philistine cursed David by his gods. And the Philistine said to David, 'Come to me, and I will give your flesh to the birds of the air and the beasts of the field!' Then David said to the Philistine, 'You come to me with a sword, with a spear, and with a javelin. But I come to you in the name of the Lord of hosts, the God of the armies of Israel, whom you have defied. This day the Lord will deliver you into my hand, and I will strike you and take your head from you. And this day I will give the carcasses of the camp of the Philistines to the birds of the air and the wild beasts of the earth, that all the earth may know that there is a God in Israel. Then all this assembly shall know that the Lord does not save with sword and spear; for the battle is the Lord's, and He will give you into our hands.' So it was, when the Philistine arose and came and drew near to meet David, that David hurried and ran toward the army to meet the Philistine. Then David put his hand in his bag and took out a stone; and he slung it and struck the Philistine in his forehead, so that the stone sank into his forehead, and he fell on his face to the earth. So David prevailed over the Philistine with a sling and a stone, and struck the Philistine and killed him. But there was no sword in the hand of David. Therefore David ran and stood over the Philistine, took his sword and drew it out of its sheath and killed him, and cut off his head with

> *it. And when the Philistines saw that their champion was dead, they fled." —1 Samuel 17:41–51 (NKJV)*

During one prayer and fasting exercise, shortly after I began speaking against the fears in my life, I was alone in my office at my new location. One of those days, I decided to spend my lunch break in prayers. I hadn't fully begun praying when I heard, "When are you going to move?" The voice was audible enough to know it was not my imagination. I knew it was the Holy Spirit speaking to me. It was a strange question from the Holy Spirit, but I knew instantly what He meant. I asked what He needed me to do. He gave me specific instructions, and I took the steps as instructed. I knew I had to leave my paid employment of 19 years, but I was ready to follow the path He had set for me. At this point, the voice of fears and limiting beliefs were so minimized that they no longer affected me. I had magnified the Words of the Lord in my mind and subconscious mind, thus making me take corresponding actions as instructed.

As children of God, our paths continue to shine brighter and brighter as we take those actions. Just like babies learning to walk, we take small steps one at a time, and our feet get stronger to maintain balance and stability. "But the path of the just is like the shining sun, That shines ever brighter unto the perfect day." (Proverbs 4:18, NKJV)

As I prepared this chapter and asked God about taking action, He said, "When you take action, you are walking in obedience." So, there is a connection between obedience and action-taking. If you're speaking, and you're not taking actions as instructed by the Lord, then you are acting in disobedience. It's time to take action. It's time to move in that direction.

You may be asking yourself, "What if I do all these, and I am yet to receive an instruction from the Lord?" First, you must know that the Bible is God speaking to you. Many times, we anticipate receiving an inspirational word from the Lord. However, the principles to follow are written in the Word of God. The Bible is God's sure Word of prophecy. We must test words received through revelational knowledge to determine their alignment with the scriptures to avoid being a victim of deception.

> *"And so we have the prophetic word confirmed, which you do well to heed as a light that shines in a dark place, until the day dawns and the morning star rises in your hearts; knowing this first, that no prophecy of Scripture is of any private [j]interpretation, for prophecy never came by the will of man, but holy men of God spoke as they were moved by the Holy Spirit." —2 Peter 1:19-21 (NKJV)*

You must be willing to wait for it patiently and not give up speaking. Remember Daniel in Babylon? For 21 days, he was praying and talking to God about the Israelites in Babylon. God heard him from the first day, and an angel was dispatched to bring the answer to him, but he hadn't received a word from the Lord on the action to take. He didn't quit until the angel bringing the answer came to him. The ruler's spirit over the territory delayed the angel. He continued to make his petition to the Lord.

> *"Then he said to me, 'Do not fear, Daniel, for from the first day that you set your heart to understand, and to*

> *humble yourself before your God, your words were heard; and I have come because of your words. But the prince of the kingdom of Persia withstood me twenty-one days; and behold, Michael, one of the chief princes, came to help me, for I had been left alone there with the kings of Persia. Now I have come to make you understand what will happen to your people in the latter days, for the vision refers to many days yet to come."* —Daniel 10:12-14 (NKJV)

Jesus also, in His parable of the persistent widow, instructs us not to give up until we have received what we desire. Giving up is aborting the process prematurely before you receive the Word.

> *"Then Jesus told his disciples a parable to show them that they should always pray and not give up. He said: 'In a certain town there was a judge who neither feared God nor cared what people thought. And there was a widow in that town who kept coming to him with the plea, "Grant me justice against my adversary." For some time he refused. But finally he said to himself, "Even though I don't fear God or care what people think, yet because this widow keeps bothering me, I will see that she gets justice, so that she won't eventually come and attack me!"' And the Lord said, 'Listen to what the unjust judge says. And will not God bring about justice for his chosen ones, who cry out to him day and night? Will he keep putting them off? I tell you, he will see that they get justice, and quickly. However, when the Son of Man comes, will he find faith on the earth?'"* —Luke 18:1-8 (NIV)

In addition to staying persistent in your declarations, develop a heart of praise and gratitude to God. As I conclude this chapter, I encourage you to take action as instructed by the Lord.

Taking Actions

Taking action is vital to overcoming limitations and obtaining God's promises.

What is the Lord reminding you in this season?

Taking Actions

What has the Lord said to you since you began the challenge concerning each fear you listed?

Taking Actions

What actions are you ready and willing to take at this time?

_____

_____

_____

_____

_____

_____

_____

_____

_____

_____

When do you plan to begin taking these actions?

My Notes

CHAPTER 6
Pulling Out the Weeds

In this chapter, we will be looking at pulling out the weeds. To weed out means to remove something that is not wanted. It is eliminating something that could negatively affect the result or efficacy of a desired outcome. A weed, according to an online dictionary, is a wild plant growing where it is not wanted and in competition with cultivated plants. Essentially, a weed is any plant growing where it's not needed. In addition, "to compete with the cultivated plants" means that it is taking up space and part of the nutrients meant for the cultivated plant, which ultimately hinders the growth and full maturity of the plant. Sometimes, it takes up all the nutrients, leading to the plant's premature death. Concerning speaking against fears and limiting beliefs, weeding out implies eliminating behaviors, attitudes, relationships, associations, and anything that will devalue and reduce the efficacy of the Word of God in your life. For the Word of God to fully manifest and bring forth fruits in your life, you need to uproot whatever competes with it.

Jesus used the parable of the sower as an illustration to help us understand the adverse effects of these weeds in the life of a believer. As stated by Jesus Christ in this parable, the different kinds of soil represent the heart of men, while the seeds in his hand are God's Word. He described four different soils. The first soil is the wayside soil. The second is the rocky ground. The third one is the thorny field. The fourth one is the one that was good soil.

> *"That same day Jesus went out of the house and sat by the lake. Such large crowds gathered around him that he got into a boat and sat in it while all the people stood on the shore. Then he told them many things in parables, saying: 'A farmer went out to sow his seed. As he was scattering the seed, some fell along the path, and the birds came and ate it up. Some fell on rocky places where it did not have much soil. It sprang up quickly, because the soil was shallow. But when the sun came up, the plants were scorched, and they withered because they had no root. Other seed fell among thorns, which grew up and choked the plants. Still other seed fell on good soil, where it produced a crop—a hundred, sixty or thirty times what was sown.'"* —Matthew 13:1–8 (NIV)

In His explanation to His disciples, when asked, Jesus Christ said that those different fields are the hearts of men, and the seed is the Word of God. As you begin speaking the Word of God against the fears in your life from the beginning of this book, you are sowing seeds. The seeds go down into your heart and begin to grow. In speaking against fears and limiting beliefs, you are planting new seeds of the Word of God into your heart.

You may ask, "Why weed out?" I live in Central Illinois, USA, and there are a lot of farmlands around me. I watch the farmers carefully prepare their fields before the planting season. They bring farming equipment and tractors to till the soil, fertilize the fields, and utilize weed killers to kill the weeds before dropping the seeds into the ground for them to grow. This is done so that the desired harvest is achieved.

In the parable of the sower above, Jesus stated that the first soil did not receive the Word of God because it was just the wayside, also known as the pathway. The enemy takes advantage and quickly snatches it away due to a lack of understanding. This kind of heart is so consumed with life issues that there is no room for the Word of God.

> *"Listen then to what the parable of the sower means: When anyone hears the message about the kingdom and does not understand it, the evil one comes and snatches away what was sown in their heart. This is the seed sown along the path." —Matthew 13:18-19 (NIV)*

The second soil received the seeds joyfully because it had room for God's Word to grow. However, the impediments outweigh God's Word, causing the Word to die quickly.

> *"The seed falling on rocky ground refers to someone who hears the word and at once receives it with joy. But since they have no root, they last only a short time. When trouble or persecution comes because of the word, they quickly fall away." —Matthew 13:20-21 (NIV)*

The third soil received the seeds but had so many concerns and worries about life that they choked the Word of God from becoming fruitful. The Word grew, but the worries of life prevented the Word from bearing fruits, making the Word of God of no effect on the individual's life.

> *"The seed falling among the thorns refers to someone who hears the word, but the worries of this life and the deceitfulness of wealth choke the word, making it unfruitful." —Matthew 13:22 (NIV)*

Sometimes our hearts are so crowded with worries and life issues that they prevent the Word of God from bringing forth its fruit in our lives. These worries are restrictions that need to be uprooted in other to achieve fruitfulness. They are occupying space and attempting to grow where they are not wanted. If left alone, they will choke the Word of God. These worries do not add anything good to your life.

> *"Therefore I tell you, do not worry about your life, what you will eat or drink; or about your body, what you will wear. Is not life more than food, and the body more than clothes? Look at the birds of the air; they do not sow or reap or store away in barns, and yet your heavenly Father feeds them. Are you not much more valuable than they? Can any one of you by worrying add a single hour to your life?" —Matthew 6:25-27 (NIV)*

After years of living a life filled with fear and worries, I realized that worrying was not adding any value to my life but was preventing God's Word from bearing fruit. When I gained this understanding, I used the steps in this book to overcome each life situation as it presents itself.

Your goal is to see God's word produce fruits in your life just as Jesus illustrated about the fourth soil. You must pull the weeds out for God's word to produce fruits.

> *"But the seed falling on good soil refers to someone who hears and understands the word. This is the one who produces a crop, yielding a hundred, sixty or thirty times what was sown." —Matthew 13:23 (NIV)*

As I began to speak God's promises over my life and visualize myself taking actions as instructed, I soon realized that one limitation I had was validation from people. Remember, in the definition of weed above, I had written that a weed is a plant that grows where it is not wanted. A weed might not necessarily be a wild plant but could be a good one growing in an unwanted field. A farmer might see soybeans growing in his cornfield, but he quickly uproots them because he doesn't want them there. Seeking validation from people is not outrightly bad in itself. Still, it can hinder your fruitfulness, especially when it does not align with their assumptions about your life's goals. Sometimes these unhealthy traits crowd and occupy the space needed for the Word of God to grow. As I continued to speak against my fears, I soon realized that seeking validation from people was preventing me from actualizing my goals.

When I approached my family and friends to tell them I was going to quit my paid job and go back to school to get their approval because the Holy Spirit had told me, many began to express their fears and concerns over my decision. These people were and are still very dear to my heart, but their worries fed my fears. I almost became discouraged, but because I had magnified the promises of God above my fears, I asked the Holy Spirit to help me. I knew I had to uproot this attitude of constantly seeking people's validation from my life, and with His help, I moved forward with this decision.

In taking action, I also began to see that there were relationships that I could no longer maintain, as they no longer fit into the pathway that God had created for me. I realized that I could not go with everyone on this new journey. Are you still seeking the validation of the people around you? Are you still fraternizing with relationships that are choking the Word of God? Do you struggle with behaviors that make the Word of God fruitless? You need to remove all these impediments for the Word to be fruitful.

Jesus Christ told the teachers of the law in his days on earth that they were handing over the traditions of men to the people and making the Word of God of no effect in their lives. You could also be embracing laws and principles of the world's systems that have reduced the efficacy of God's Word.

> *"And he continued, 'You have a fine way of setting aside the commands of God in order to observe your own traditions! For Moses said, "Honor your father and mother," and, "Anyone who curses their father or mother is to be put to death." But you say that if anyone declares that what might have been used to help their father or mother is Cor-*

> *ban (that is, devoted to God) then you no longer let them do anything for their father or mother. Thus you nullify the word of God by your tradition that you have handed down. And you do many things like that.'" —Mark 7:9-13 (NIV)*

Perhaps, you are struggling with doubts or double-mindedness. One minute you are speaking God's promises, and when faced with those challenges again, you begin to question the efficacy of God's Word, just like the second soil in the parable of the sower mentioned above. God's Word will wither when you do not get rid of doubts and double-mindedness.

> *"If any of you lacks wisdom, let him ask of God, who gives to all liberally and without reproach, and it will be given to him. But let him ask in faith, with no doubting, for he who doubts is like a wave of the sea driven and tossed by the wind. For let not that man suppose that he will receive anything from the Lord; he is a double-minded man, unstable in all his ways." —James 1:5-8 (NKJV)*

Other times, these restrictions are negative behaviors and attitudes that work against the Word of God. These attitudes will choke like thorns and prevent the promises of God from actualizing in your life. It would be best if you got rid of them.

> *"So put to death the sinful, earthly things lurking within you. Have nothing to do with sexual immorality, impurity, lust, and evil desires. Don't be greedy, for a greedy person is an idolater, worshiping the things of this world. Because of these sins, the anger of God is coming. You used to do these*

> *things when your life was still part of this world. But now is the time to get rid of anger, rage, malicious behavior, slander, and dirty language. Don't lie to each other, for you have stripped off your old sinful nature and all its wicked deeds. Put on your new nature, and be renewed as you learn to know your Creator and become like him."* —Colossians 3:5–10 (NLT)

To overcome the fears in your life and forge ahead, you must be willing to get rid of the hindrances in your way and take action according to God's promises. There is hope, joy, and fulfillment as you journey.

> *"Therefore we also, since we are surrounded by so great a cloud of witnesses, let us lay aside every weight, and the sin which so easily ensnares us, and let us run with endurance the race that is set before us, looking unto Jesus, the author and finisher of our faith, who for the joy that was set before Him endured the cross, despising the shame, and has sat down at the right hand of the throne of God."* —Hebrews 12:1–2 (NKJV)

Weeding out could be painful, but greater joy and glory are ahead. What are those things that you are holding on to? What weight are you still carrying that need to be set aside? What character traits do you need to put off or get rid of? Your weight could be constant validation of humans or even trying to please everyone. In saying yes to people, you may end up with many emotional dilemmas, which can keep you constantly in despair of who you are and your self-worth.

One of the excuses that I gave God after receiving the instruction from my company to relocate to a part of my country was the lack of support for my children and me. I remember making my case for why it wasn't a good idea. Then Holy Spirit told me, "You are too concerned about mundane things." I was surprised when He said that because, due to my constant worrying, I thought the responsibility of support and care for my family lies with me. I had to get rid of that attitude and trust that God's promises for me include provision and support.

Other times, the Holy Spirit had to point out the pride in me that was a source of hindrance in my marital relationship. Other times, He showed me elements of anger I had toward my husband which were evident in my passive-aggressive tendencies toward him. All these negative behaviors were weeds that gave the enemy foothold in my marriage. I spent time weeding out these negative behaviors and still do as the Lord points them out.

Weeding out is removing those hindrances from your life. They do not produce any good results and also affect your fruitfulness. What do you need to weed out as you progress with your life?

This chapter will create some unease in you because of some old habits or relationships that the Holy Spirit requires you to eliminate. I encourage you to trust Him as He leads you and rely on Him for strength and grace to be a doer of His Word.

Pulling Out the Weeds

"Now the works of the flesh are evident, which are: adultery, fornication, uncleanness, lewdness, idolatry, sorcery, hatred, contentions, jealousies, outbursts of wrath, selfish ambitions, dissensions, heresies, envy, murders, drunkenness, revelries, and the like; of which I tell you beforehand, just as I also told you in time past, that those who practice such things will not inherit the kingdom of God." —Galatians 5:19–21 (NKJV)

What do I need to weed out in this season?

Sinful Nature

_____

_____

_____

_____

_____

_____

_____

_____

Negative Character Traits

"Let all bitterness, wrath, anger, clamor, and evil speaking be put away from you, with all malice. 32 And be kind to one another, tenderhearted, forgiving one another, even as God in Christ forgave you." — Ephesians 4:31–32 (NKJV)

What do I need to weed out in this season?

Negative Language/Conversations

Limiting Beliefs/Mindset about myself

"Do not be misled: 'Bad company corrupts good character.'" —1 Corinthians 15:33 (NIV)

Relationships

Friendships/Associations

My Notes

CHAPTER 7

Planting and Nurturing Your Seeds

We are good soil, and the Word of God sown into our hearts are the seeds. The Word sown into your hearts is required to grow to maturity. In Chapter 6, I talked about the purpose of weed, which is to devalue and reduce the efficacy of the Word of God in your life. You must pull out the weed so that the seeds sown will grow and produce fruits. The Word of God is the good seed, and your heart is the soil.

> *"But the seed falling on good soil refers to someone who hears the word and understands it. This is the one who produces a crop, yielding a hundred, sixty or thirty times what was sown." —Matthew 13:23 (NIV)*
>
> *"As newborn babes, desire the pure milk of the word, that you may grow thereby." —1 Peter 2:2 (NKJV)*

When you remove the weed, you will not leave the soil empty. If you leave the ground fallow, the weeds will grow again. When you plant the Word of God in your heart, it replaces the weed that had been uprooted. In 2 Timothy 1:7 (NKJV), the Bible says, "For God has not given us a spirit of fear, but of power and of love and of a sound mind," which implies that when you uproot fear, which is not from God, you need to plant power, love, and sound mind. All these are the seeds that God has given you, not fear.

In 1 John 4:18 (NKJV), the Bible says: "There is no fear in love; but perfect love casts out fear, because fear involves torment. But he who fears has not been made perfect in love." As you continue to sow and nurture love, it casts out the fear inside of you. Living a life of love gives you the capacity to overcome fear.

Likewise, you replace anxiety with prayer, supplication, and giving thanks to God. He wants you to do this whenever you begin to experience anxiety.

> *"Be anxious for nothing, but in everything by prayer and supplication, with thanksgiving, let your requests be made known to God;* [7] *and the peace of God, which surpasses all understanding, will guard your hearts and minds through Christ Jesus." —Philippians 4:6-7 (NKJV)*

Therefore, every time your heart begins to experience fear or the limiting beliefs, you can quickly assess to see if there's any area of your life you have not been walking in love or not exercising the power God has given you. Once you identify the source, you take it to God in prayers, committing it to Him, and thank Him for answering your prayers because that is what you are required to do according to the scriptures. By taking these steps, you are not only planting the Word of God, but you are also nurturing it to maturity.

You may ask, "Why must I go through this process?" The simple answer is, so the enemy doesn't bring back the weed. You don't want to continue to fall victim to a life of perpetual fear and despair. In most situations, the individual's state worsens when the weed grows again.

> *"When an unclean spirit goes out of a man, he goes through dry places, seeking rest, and finds none. Then he says, 'I will return to my house from which I came.' And when he comes, he finds it empty, swept, and put in order. Then he goes and takes with him seven other spirits more wicked than himself, and they enter and dwell there; and the last state of that man is worse than the first. So shall it also be with this wicked generation." —Matthew 12:43-45 (NKJV)*

You must allow the Word of God to continue deep into your heart. When it does, you will bear many fruits. These fruits are the promises of God for you in every area of your life.

> *"My child, pay attention to what I say, Listen carefully to my words. Don't lose sight of them. Let them penetrate deep into your heart, for they bring life to those who find them, and healing to their whole body." —Proverbs 4:20-22 (NLT)*

> *"For I know the thoughts that I think toward you, says the Lord, thoughts of peace and not of evil, to give you a future*

and a hope. Then you will call upon Me and go and pray to Me, and I will listen to you. And you will seek Me and find Me, when you search for Me with all your heart." —Jeremiah 29:11–13 (NKJV)

"But the seed falling on good soil refers to someone who hears the word and understands it. This is the one who produces a crop, yielding a hundred, sixty or thirty times what was sown." —Matthew 13:23 (NIV)

"But if you remain in me and my words remain in you, you may ask for anything you want, and it will be granted! When you produce much fruit, you are my true disciples. This brings great glory to my Father." —John 15:7–8 (NLT)

Nurturing requires effort, time, dedication, intentionality, and diligence to achieve the required results. In other words, growth takes time. You have to keep at it and not give up or abort the process. Several times in my journey, I felt like the results were being delayed, but I didn't give up. One such occasion was when I was denied a Canadian study visa in my attempt to study for my graduate degree in counseling. I was devastated because I was prepared to leave and had informed my family, friends, and colleagues of my plans. When I received the rejection email, people began to suggest that perhaps it wasn't the will of God for me to leave. Several discouragements from friends followed, and in that season, I felt misunderstood and alone. Rather than succumb to the pressure, I continued to abide in the Word and do as the Holy Spirit instructed me. I became very intentional about overcoming the fear and limiting beliefs in my life.

During this season, the Holy Spirit gave me yet another Word to confirm that I was in the right. It was about midnight, a few days after receiving the visa denial email in January 2017. I was deep in prayers when I had an inner witness to open my Bible to the book of Isaiah. I opened Chapter 50 and began to read it. When I got to verses four and five, I heard "That's you."

> *"The Sovereign Lord has given me a well-instructed tongue to know the word that sustains the weary. He wakens me morning by morning, wakens my ear to listen like one being instructed. The Sovereign Lord has opened my ears; I have not been rebellious, I have not turned away." —Isaiah 50:4–5 (NIV)*

I began to leap for joy, knowing God's got my back. I knew that this visa denial wasn't the end of it. I was joyful, like one who had just won a massive battle because I did. It was my battle against discouragement and being stuck. I got up the next day and continued to pursue my goal.

Are you ready to overcome your life's crippling fear and limiting beliefs? Then it's time to take the needed action. Perhaps, you suffered rejection once or a couple of times; God's plan is not for you to stay defeated but to rise again and keep moving.

> *"For though the righteous fall seven times, they rise again, but the wicked stumble when calamity strikes." —Proverbs 24:16 (NIV)*

As you do all these, success is inevitable.

Planting Seeds

"A time to plant, and a time to harvest." —Ecclesiastes 3:2b

What do I need to plant this season?

1. The Word of God (seed)

2. New Belief(s)

Planting Seeds

"A time to plant, and a time to harvest." —Ecclesiastes 3:2b

What do I need to plant this season?

3. Relationships

4. Ideas/Directions/Instructions

Nurturing Your Plant for Harvest

How will I nurture the plants in this season in order to harvest? Nurturing requires effort, time, dedication, intentionality, and diligence to achieve the required results.

The Word of God (seed)

New Belief(s)

_____

_____

_____

_____

_____

_____

_____

Nurturing Your Plant for Harvest

How will I nurture the plants in this season in order to harvest? Nurturing requires effort, time, dedication, intentionality, and diligence to achieve the required results.

Relationships
_____

_____

_____

Ideas/Directions/Instructions

My Notes

CHAPTER 8

Speak and Walk in Love

Chapter 7 looked at planting and nurturing the seed—representing God's Word. You already know that the Word of God is the seed. Your heart or the condition of our heart is the soil for the Word of God. Likewise, the Word of God can only produce a harvest when our hearts are right. This chapter will look at what really expels fear from our lives. 1 John 4:18 tells us that love is the language and action that expels fear.

> *"There is no fear in love [dread does not exist], but full-grown (complete, perfect) love turns fear out of doors and expels every trace of terror! For fear brings with it the thought of punishment, and [so] he who is afraid has not reached the full maturity of love [is not yet grown into love's complete perfection]."* —1 John 4:18 (AMPC)

Just as the information that sowed the fears came into our hearts, the information that expels the fears and sows love can also come into our hearts. Therefore, the antidote for fear is to speak and walk in love.

When you receive the Word of God into your heart, you need to anchor it on God's love. The Word of God you have listed as you continue to progress in this journey must be anchored on God's love. An anchor "is something that serves to hold an object firmly" (Merriam-Webster Dictionary).

God's love will hold you firmly rooted so you are not moved, discouraged, or blown away when adverse conditions arise. When you are strong, no matter the storms of life, it will keep you standing.

> *"Then Christ will make his home in your hearts as you trust in him. Your roots will grow down into God's love and keep you strong." —Ephesians*

God's Nature and Personality is Love.

> *"Dear friends, let us continue to love one another, for love comes from God. Anyone who loves is a child of God and knows God." —1 John*

You need to know that as a child of God, you are born of love. You have God's nature of love inside of you. You might not have lived with this understanding and reality, but it is in you.

As such, He wants you to exhibit this nature because this will expel all the fears that the enemy tries to use to prevent you from walking in your potential and destiny.

> *"Dear friends, since God loved us that much, we surely ought to love each other. No one has ever seen God. But if we love each other, God lives in us, and his love is brought*

> *to full expression in us." —1 John 4:11-12 (NLT)*

If you walk in love, the nature of God in you will be evident to the world. To walk in love is a process and journey. Apostle Paul calls it the more excellent way (1 Corinthians 12:31, KJV). He went further to list the nature of love and the characteristics of love. In this journey to overcoming fear and limiting beliefs, living a life of love and anchoring ourselves in God's love will give us victory. Your actions, attitudes, and behaviors will be assessed through God's love.

A few years ago, I remember arguing with my husband over a financial decision that he was about to take. I didn't have peace over the decision, and it required us to use some bonus money that I had just received from my company. My husband was in graduate school in the United Kingdom at that time. Still, he was also trying to complete a business proposal to support the family financially. I was very upset about it, and for a whole day, we argued back and forth, with no one yielding to the other. During my prayer time the following morning, the Holy Spirit began to correct me. He said I was prideful and arrogant in my conversation with my husband. He pointed me to how I didn't respond in love because I told him I worked for the money. I repented and asked for forgiveness from the Lord. I called my husband and apologized to him too. I was afraid to loose money, and my fear made me act with pride toward my husband.

> *"Love endures long and is patient and kind; love never is envious nor boils over with jealousy, is not boastful or vainglorious, does not display itself haughtily. It is not conceited (arrogant and inflated with pride); it is not rude*

(unmannerly) and does not act unbecomingly. Love (God's love in us) does not insist on its own rights or its own way, for it is not self-seeking; it is not touchy or fretful or resentful; it takes no account of the evil done to it [it pays no attention to a suffered wrong]. It does not rejoice at injustice and unrighteousness, but rejoices when right and truth prevail. Love bears up under anything and everything that comes, is ever ready to believe the best of every person, its hopes are fadeless under all circumstances, and it endures everything [without weakening]. Love never fails [never fades out or becomes obsolete or comes to an end]. As for prophecy (the gift of interpreting the divine will and purpose), it will be fulfilled and pass away; as for tongues, they will be destroyed and cease; as for knowledge, it will pass away [it will lose its value and be superseded by truth]." —1 Corinthians 13:4–8 (AMPC)

So, how does love expel fear?

- Love will help you to do the opposite of what fear wants you to do.

The brothers of Joseph acted out of fear and jealousy that he would someday lead them and sold him as an enslaved person. Joseph, on the other hand, did the opposite.

"But don't be upset, and don't be angry with yourselves for selling me to this place. It was God who sent me here ahead of you to preserve your lives." —Genesis 45:5 (NLT)

- Love strengthens your heart and emboldens you to stand against fear.

"And may the Lord make your love for one another and for all people grow and overflow, just as our love for you overflows. May he, as a result, make your hearts strong, blameless, and holy as you stand before God our Father when our Lord Jesus comes again with all his holy people. Amen." —1 Thessalonians 3:12-13 (NLT)

- Love gives you the power to overcome fear and limiting beliefs. You can resist the enemy because you walk in love. Nothing is as enriching as knowing that God's love gives you the power to overcome fear.

"For God has not given us a spirit of fear, but of power and of love and of a sound mind." —2 Timothy 1:7 (NKJV)

- Love enables you to obey God's Word and not fear. It will make you a doer of God's Word.

"But if anyone obeys his word, love for God is truly made complete in them. This is how we know we are in him." —1 John 2:5 (NIV)

- Love illuminates your path. It gives you the ability to see from God's perspective.

"Anyone who loves their brother and sister lives in the light, and there is nothing in them to make them stumble. But anyone who hates a brother or sister is in the darkness and walks around in the darkness. They do not know where they are going, because the darkness has blinded them." —1 John 2:10-11 (NIV)

What is the love of God teaching you in this journey? I desire to see the children of God walk in victory over everything that limits their potential. The enemy plans to hinder the children of God from achieving this goal, just as the Word says:

> *"The thief comes only in order to steal and kill and destroy. I came that they may have and enjoy life, and have it in abundance [to the full, till it overflows]." —John 10:10 (AMP)*

The plan and will of God is for us to enjoy the abundance of life that Jesus Christ has obtained through His death and resurrection for us. Walking in His love, doing His will, and anchoring ourselves in God's love gives us power over fear and limiting beliefs.

My Notes

Appendices

While putting together this book and the worksheets, I shared some common fears among humanity, some of which I experienced on my journey.

Fear of Being Misunderstood

I studied the life of David and his character; one of the obstacles he faced was the misunderstanding of his motive by his family. His siblings misunderstood him when they saw him at the battleground. Likewise, Moses faced similar opposition when he rescued an Israelite from an Egyptian and killed the Egyptian. His action was misunderstood by the Israelites when he tried to intervene the next time he saw two Israelites fighting. As a result, he fled Egypt for fear of being killed by Pharaoh.

Both men had different outcomes at the onset of their opposition:

1. David's oldest brother, Elian, was trying to shut him up, but he didn't succumb to him and went ahead to kill Goliath (1 Kings 17)

2. Moses ran, and he became a shepherd for 40 years (Exodus 2)

In David's story, he didn't allow the negative talks from his siblings to hinder his decision. At the same time, Moses ran away for fear of being killed by the king. Could the good things you've done have been misunderstood and resulted in you quitting the good things you are destined to do, or perhaps you stopped following your dreams? My encouragement for you is that it's time to pick up from where you left off. It's time to stop being afraid because you were misunderstood and labeled. It's time to speak the mind of God and the message He has given to you for your generation.

Today, I encourage you with the scriptures below:

> *"Don't be afraid, for I am with you. Don't be discouraged, for I am your God. I will strengthen you and help you. I will hold you up with my victorious right hand." —Isaiah 41:10 (NLT)*

> *"'Be strong and of good courage, do not fear nor be afraid of them; for the Lord your God, He is the One who goes with you. He will not leave you nor forsake you.' And the Lord, He is the One who goes before you. He will be with you, He will not leave you nor forsake you; do not fear nor be dismayed." —Deuteronomy 31:6, 8 (NKJV)*

Prayer: Today, I pray for courage and boldness to do the things the Lord has laid upon your heart. I pray for healing from where you have been betrayed that left you with wounds in your heart. I pray that you may be conscious that the Lord is holding your hands, and you need not be afraid in Jesus' name. Amen

Fear of Total Surrender

For some, it is ultimately yielding to God that is the fear. Some fear that God will lead them on a path they might not like or even through pathways that many will misunderstand or mock. They fear that if they say yes, they no longer control the outcome. In the process, they settle for less or even ask the Lord to endorse the alternate path they chose for themselves. God created you and has a glorious destiny for you, just as He told Jeremiah.

> "The Lord gave me this message: "I knew you before I formed you in your mother's womb. Before you were born I set you apart and appointed you as my prophet to the nations." —Jeremiah 1:4–5 (NLT)

He knew you before you became a living soul, and he already appointed you for that assignment or your purpose.

> "'For I know the plans I have for you,' says the Lord. 'They are plans for good and not for disaster, to give you a future and a hope.'" —Jeremiah 29:11 (NLT)

His plans are always good for His children. The prophet Jonah ran away when God asked him to go to Nineveh; he boarded a ship to Tarshish. He knew he couldn't control the outcome of his prophesy to the people.

> "Now the word of the Lord came unto Jonah the son of Amittai, saying, Arise, go to Nineveh, that great city, and cry against it; for their wickedness is come up before me. But Jonah rose up to flee unto Tarshish from the presence of the Lord, and went down to Joppa; and he found a ship going to Tarshish: so he paid the fare thereof, and went down into it, to go with them unto Tarshish from the pres-

ence of the Lord." —Jonah 1:1-3 (KJV)

I started speaking against my fears in February 2016, and in May of that same year, while I was praying and fasting, the Lord spoke to me. I remember being alone in my office when I heard the voice of the Holy Spirit telling me it was time to move. I received the instructions with joy. However, I didn't ask "Where?" When I told my husband what my plans were, he said, "Why not USA?" I didn't accept it. I remember saying "God spoke to me," and I knew what I was doing. I attempted to go to Canada, but it didn't work. I made the second attempt; it didn't work. I lost money and time. People started questioning my motive for wanting to leave. I had my reasons and feared God saying "Go to the USA." I had my conclusions. Again, my husband said, "Why not USA?" So, I returned to God, and I remember that I prayed a prayer of surrender at midnight.

> *"He went on a little farther and bowed with his face to the ground, praying, 'My Father! If it is possible, let this cup of suffering be taken away from me. Yet I want your will to be done, not mine.'" —Matthew 26:39 (NLT)*

Jesus surrendered to God's will (Hebrews 12:1-2). There was a joy set before Christ. His surrendering to God's will brought many sons and daughters to God, which includes you and me.

I wouldn't be doing this today if I didn't surrender. There's a difference between giving up and surrendering to God's will. What happens is, people, instead, give up because it's not working as they envisioned or didn't work as they planned but not in total surrender to God's original design for them.

So, as you go through this journey, I encourage you to look at the areas of fear in your life and ask the Lord what you are holding on to that you need to surrender. Is it your future, career, family, marriage, relationship, finances, children, and others? God is calling you to a deeper walk and intimacy.

Prayer: Lord, I pray that You open my eyes to see the areas of my life where I'm not in total surrender to Your will and give me the grace to be obedient. In Jesus' name. Amen.

Fear of Inadequacy toward achieving your goals or assignment - Imposter Syndrome

According to Collins dictionary, if someone has feelings of inadequacy, they feel they do not have the qualities and abilities necessary to do something or to cope with life in general. Inadequacy is a feeling of incompetence, unskillfulness, and deficiency in doing something. When you feel inadequate, you tell yourself you are not good enough. This fear is also called Imposter Syndrome. This feeling is prevalent among humans. Remember I said I had so many fears about my life and situation? I struggled with this fear for years until I began to speak against it. Several patriarchs of faith that we discuss in the Bible also experienced the same. When God called Moses in Exodus 3 to deliver the children of Israel, he gave God excuses. In Exodus 3:11 (KJV), Moses questioned why he should be given the assignment: "And Moses said unto God, Who am I, that I should go unto Pharaoh, and that I should bring forth the children of Israel out of Egypt?" In Exodus 4:1 (KJV), he said the elders of Israel wouldn't believe him: "And Moses answered and said, But, behold, they will not believe me, nor hearken unto my voice: for they will say, The Lord hath not appeared unto thee." In Exodus 4:10 (KJV), Moses continued to give God reasons why he wasn't qualified for that assignment by expressing that he wasn't eloquent: "And Moses said unto the Lord, O my Lord, I am not eloquent, neither heretofore, nor since thou hast spoken unto thy servant: but I am slow of speech, and of a slow tongue." He made excuses until God said that Aaron, his brother, would be his spokesperson.

In Judges 6, Gideon gave reasons why he wasn't fit for the position to rescue the Israelites from the Midianites. His excuse was that he was the least in his father's house. "And he said unto him, Oh my Lord, wherewith shall I save Israel? behold, my family is poor in Manasseh, and I am the least in my father's house." (Judges 6:15, KJV)

Jeremiah said that he was only a child when God called him to be a prophet. "Then said I, Ah, Lord God! behold, I cannot speak: for I am a child." (Jeremiah 1:6, KJV)

This kind of fear continues to show you images of someone incapable of doing the assignment God has given them or even walking in the path of their destiny. A common saying is that God does not call the qualified but qualifies the called. David was only a shepherd boy when God called and anointed him to be king over Israel. Gideon was a timid farmer when God called him to be a judge. When Jesus picked His disciples, the first four were unlearned men who only knew about fishing. He called Peter the rock upon which the church will be built.

> *"Remember, dear brothers and sisters, that few of you were wise in the world's eyes or powerful or wealthy when God called you. Instead, God chose things the world considers foolish to shame those who think they are wise. And he chose things that are powerless to shame those who are powerful. God chose things despised by the world, counted as nothing at all, and used them to bring what the world considers important to nothing. As a result, no one can ever boast in the presence of God." —1 Corinthians 1:26-29 (NLT)*

The system of the world only calls the qualified because they need to see your resume and experiences before you are employed. However, with God, it is so different. He calls you first, then takes you through the qualifications. It is God who called you and chose you. If He gave you that instruction, His presence and power will back you up to fulfillment.

So, today, I encourage you to speak against this fear of inadequacy by telling it, "I am the called according to His promise. God called me and has qualified me. I make every bold step toward doing what He's asked me to do in Jesus' name. Amen."

Fear of Loosing what you have and Getting Stuck

This fear is associated with giving up something valuable or your last means of livelihood. Elijah was sent to that widow of Zarepheth to take care of him. He got there and asked for a meal. She responded that it was her last meal and had planned to eat it with her son, then both would die afterward.

> *"Arise, get thee to Zarephath, which belongeth to Zidon, and dwell there: behold, I have commanded a widow woman there to sustain thee. So he arose and went to Zarephath. And when he came to the gate of the city, behold, the widow woman was there gathering of sticks: and he called to her, and said, Fetch me, I pray thee, a little water in a vessel, that I may drink. And as she was going to fetch it, he called to her, and said, Bring me, I pray thee, a morsel of bread in thine hand. And she said, As the Lord thy God liveth, I have not a cake, but an handful of meal in a barrel, and a little oil in a cruse: and, behold, I am gathering two sticks, that I may go in and dress it for me and my son, that we may eat it, and die. And Elijah said unto her, fear not; go and do as thou hast said: but make me thereof a little cake first, and bring it unto me, and after make for thee and for thy son." —1 Kings 17:9–13 (KJV)*

It was their last meal; however, she obeyed the prophet, and God sustained them through the famine.

> *"For thus saith the Lord God of Israel, The barrel of meal shall not waste, neither shall the cruse of oil fail, until the day that the Lord sendeth rain upon the earth. And she went and did according to the saying of Elijah: and she, and he, and her house, did eat many days. And the barrel of meal wasted not, neither did the cruse of oil fail, according to the word of the Lord, which he spake by Elijah." —1 Kings 17:14–16 (KJV)*

Another example in the Bible is Job. He was a man that was devoted to God. He reverenced God and did well in his life.

> *"In the land of Uz there lived a man whose name was Job. This man was blameless and upright; he feared God and shunned evil." —Job 1:1 (NIV)*

However, he had fear of losing his children and wealth. As a result, he would make sacrifices on behalf of his children whenever they held a feast. He perpetuated this fear according to his confession when he lost all his children.

> *"His sons used to hold feasts in their homes on their birthdays, and they would invite their three sisters to eat and drink with them. When a period of feasting had run its course, Job would make arrangements for them to be purified. Early in the morning he would sacrifice a burnt offering for each of them, thinking, 'Perhaps my children have sinned and cursed God in their hearts.' This was Job's regular custom." —Job 1:4-5 (NIV)*

> *"What I always feared has happened to me. What I dreaded has come true. I have no peace, no quietness. I have no rest; only trouble comes." —Job 3:25-26 (NLT)*

A confident, wealthy young man came to Jesus to ask Him what he needed to do to have eternal life. Jesus asked him to sell everything he owned, give the money to the poor, and follow him. This young man left sad because he had great possessions and couldn't part with them.

"Someone came to Jesus with this question: 'Teacher, what good deed must I do to have eternal life?' 'Why ask me about what is good?' Jesus replied. 'There is only One who is good. But to answer your question—if you want to receive eternal life, keep the commandments.' 'Which ones?' the man asked. And Jesus replied: 'You must not murder. You must not commit adultery. You must not steal. You must not testify falsely. Honor your father and mother. Love your neighbor as yourself.' 'I've obeyed all these commandments,' the young man replied. 'What else must I do?' Jesus told him, 'If you want to be perfect, go and sell all your possessions and give the money to the poor, and you will have treasure in heaven. Then come, follow me.' But when the young man heard this, he went away sad, for he had many possessions. Then Jesus said to his disciples, 'I tell you the truth, it is very hard for a rich person to enter the Kingdom of Heaven. I'll say it again—it is easier for a camel to go through the eye of a needle than for a rich person to enter the Kingdom of God!' The disciples were astounded. 'Then who in the world can be saved?' they asked. Jesus looked at them intently and said, 'Humanly speaking, it is impossible. But with God everything is possible.'" — Matthew 19:16–22 (NKJV)

In these three illustrations, we see that fear can make one hold on to things that God wants us to release. When the widow obeyed the prophet, she didn't lack food till the famine ended. Job regained his sons and daughters because he was being tested without knowledge. The rich young man was sad about giving up his possessions, and nothing further was written about him being a follower of Jesus Christ.

I remember when my company transferred me to Rivers State from Lagos State, Nigeria, away from their headquarters. I had so many reasons why it wasn't my best idea to go. I prayed against going to that location. I couldn't imagine leaving my extended family members, social support, and even our new home barely a few months after moving in. I was trying to lobby my way out of it but decided to pray again—but this time, for God to speak His mind and intervene. Then the Holy Spirit said, "You are too concerned about mundane things." He indeed wanted me to go. He promised to care for us and even give me a hundredfold whatever I thought I would lose. He reminded me of this passage as confirmation:

> *"Then Peter answered and said to Him, 'See, we have left all and followed You. Therefore what shall we have?' So Jesus said to them, 'Assuredly I say to you, that in the regeneration, when the Son of Man sits on the throne of His glory, you who have followed Me will also sit on twelve thrones, judging the twelve tribes of Israel. And everyone who has left houses or brothers or sisters or father or mother or wife or children or lands, for My name's sake, shall receive a hundredfold and inherit eternal life. But many who are first will be last, and the last first.'"* —Matthew 19:27-30 (NKJV)

Indeed He was true to His promise. I'm grateful that the journey that led to this book and many other things I've achieved today began back then. Fear will hinder you from reaching your full potential if you constantly yield to it. God's plan for you is to live a life of hope and fulfillment. He will always back His Word to fulfill as you yield to Him.

> *"'For I know the plans I have for you,' declares the Lord, 'plans to prosper you and not to harm you, plans to give you hope and a future.'" —Jeremiah 29:11 (NIV)*

Prayer: Lord, I ask that You search my heart and reveal what I'm holding on to due to fear of losing it. Give me the grace to give it up and follow the ways and path You have set for me in Jesus' name. Amen

My Notes

Call To Action

Congratulations! You have made it to the end of this book. However, your journey begins here. I encourage you to take the steps detailed in this book. Locate and speak the promises of God. Take those bold steps in alignment with God's promises. Weed out all impediments and begin your journey by planting and nurturing your goals and desires.

Testimonials

I have been so blessed by Lola and her "Speaking Against Fears" challenge. This challenge could not have come at a better time. I was struggling with severe postpartum depression and anxiety, and my fears were crippling me. The enemy had even convinced me that I could not be a child of God since I was struggling so much. This fear led me to avoid God because I was ashamed for not having it all together. Lola's teaching helped me not only identify the fears and lies I was believing but empowered me to use my mouth to speak against them with the truth of God's Word. Lola is an anointed teacher and counselor, and you can tell she deeply cares for those God has put in her path. I am forever grateful for her obedience to the LORD to help believers know their identity in Christ and how to walk in the freedom Christ died for them to have. This challenge reminded me of the Truth and enabled me to find deliverance from my fears in some of my darkest days. "I sought the LORD, and he answered me and delivered me from all my fears" (Psalms 34:4).

Kristen Gurule, TN, USA

I was so blessed by Lola's Warrior Heart Challenge "Speaking Against Fears." I was coming from a place of great change in my life, and I was feeling defeated on many levels. This challenge was just what I needed and helped me to see the effect fear was having on me and how fear became a driving factor that wasn't from God. She first had us identify what our fears were and speak against them with scripture. This was revealing on many levels. It also helped me to recognize negative self-talk and speak words of love, kindness, patience, and grace over myself. I have known Lola for quite a few years now and have been so blessed by her Godly strength and courage, her teaching, and how the Holy Spirit works through her to speak to me and others.

Cindy Smith, TN, USA

I was introduced to Lola Lawal by my dearest friend and sister of over 20 years at a crucial point in my life when my biggest treasure—my family—was on the verge of collapse. Her calm demeanor, the depth of her wisdom, and her knowledge of scriptures in backing up her counsel filled my heart with hope and, by extension, my home, as I started putting all I had learnt into practice. Two years under her tutelage and guidance have been nothing short of spectacular. I have experienced massive growth personally and in my marriage. There has been a tremendous shift in my life evidenced by my level of confidence, career growth, and walk with God. Many things set Mrs. Lawal apart, but I'll mention one, which is her commitment to the holistic growth (spirit, mind, and body) of an individual through the guidance of the Holy Spirit. She is one professional therapist that stands out and stands tall. I would recommend her 100X over.

Jumoke Ogunleye, ON, CANADA

Omolola Lawal and I have come a long way, and I can attest that she is a very strong woman of faith, a prayer warrior, a therapist, a counselor, a loving wife, and a fantastic mother. When she told me about the "Speaking Against Fears" challenge, I keyed into it because I have been under her tutelage before and knew it was going to bless me. As at that time, I was battling with a lot of fears. The challenge did not only help me to identify my fears but also taught me to speak against them and also helped me to weed out unwanted elements in my life.

I strongly recommend this book for all and sundry because it will be of great benefit.

Temitope Oluwakemi Oladapo, LA, NIGERIA

I joined the "Speaking Against Fears" challenge by Lola Lawal at a time I was struggling with fear of the unknown. One of the ways the challenge helped me was being able to name the fear. I had to ask myself, "What is it that I am afraid of?" After identifying it, I called it out and then began to speak against it. That challenge was incredibly impactful for me. It came at such a time in the season of my life when I needed to really not act out of fear but out of love. The scriptures and the prayers were powerful. The prayers really helped me to put things into practice, and not just receiving words. I also really enjoyed the fact that we had a Facebook group and shared videos on what we did individually. The worksheets were also helpful. I also loved the topic "Weeding Out." This was really good because before you can plant the new seed, you have to weed out all the things that no longer serve you. It was one of the most powerful experiences ever I've had spiritually and has really helped me to reinforce my foundation in knowing who I am.

Esther Oni Hephzibah, NB, CANADA

I had the rare privilege of being on Mrs. Omolola Lawal's program "Speaking Against Fears," which was an impactful and insightful encounter, confronting my fears with the promises of God inherent in the Word of God. Mrs. Lawal has the rare gift of teaching the Word with simplicity and power. She is a practical and pragmatic teacher of the Word who 'walks the talk' and has evidence to prove this through her life's journey. A passionate and compassionate therapist, she goes the extra mile to ensure her clients have an in-depth transformational experience. She's your go-to person for clarity on your life's journey, marriage counseling, and coaching in a non-judgemental but down-to-earth atmosphere.

Daji Mowoe-Oyetundun, SCOTLAND

I signed up for the Warrior's Heart challenge for Overcoming Fear and Limiting Beliefs at a time when I was stuck. I had relationship trauma and did not know how to move on. Every day, after meeting for the challenge, I physically felt better. Lola gave specific simple lessons that were very impactful. I went from not knowing what to do to having a clear path to take. Several things I learned in this challenge, I continue to do months later. I went on to enroll in the Warrior's Heart boot camp. Lola was a very engaged host. She took time to interact with me and all participants and met each question with wisdom and clarity. Every meeting was filled with the presence of God. When people learn new things, they say some things are taught, and some things are caught. This boot camp was the best of both. The prayer times took us right to the heart of God. Every lesson was more impactful than the last. Lola's teaching was top-notch, but her impartation was priceless. I am not the same person I was when I started. Specifically, Lola helped me to see how God's Word is specific to me. She provided a safe space to learn with other women on the same journey. I look forward to future challenges!

Jennifer Raymond, FL, USA

About The Author

Omolola (Lola) Lawal is a Christian, a licensed professional counselor in Illinois, a national certified counselor (NCC), and an author. Her passion for the spiritual and emotional well-being of individuals led her to counseling after a 19-year career in the oil and gas sector. She enjoys praying, teaching Kingdom principles, and helping Spirit-filled middle-aged women in marital crises and dissatisfaction with their life goals navigate from despair to hope and joy. She leads and participates in several women's prayer ministries and groups. She began teaching "Speaking Against Fear and Limiting Beliefs" as a virtual challenge to middle-aged women until the Holy Spirit led her to write it into a book. As a parent, Lola desires to see children discover their true identity as they develop their relationship with God as their Heavenly Father. She recently authored a daily adolescent devotional titled *Dear Heavenly Father*. She lives in Illinois, USA, with her husband of 20 years and their two sets of twins.

Email Omolola Lawal for media appearance, speaking engagements, and coaching sessions at lola@championsheartoasis.com. You can find her daily at https://www.facebook.com/lola.lawal.186, @oslawal on Instagram.

CPSIA information can be obtained
at www.ICGtesting.com
Printed in the USA
LVHW071525170723
752375LV00015B/390